Library of Philosophy and Religion

General Editor: **John Hick**, Fellow of the Institute for Advanced Study in the Humanities, University of Birmingham

This series of books explores contemporary religious understandings of humanity and the universe. The books contribute to various aspects of the continuing dialogues between religion and philosophy, between scepticism and faith, and between the different religions and ideologies. The authors represent a correspondingly wide range of viewpoints. Some of the books in the series are written for the general educated public and others for a more specialized philosophical or theological readership.

Selected titles:

Masao Abe
BUDDHISM AND INTERFAITH DIALOGUE
ZEN AND WESTERN THOUGHT

Dan Cohn-Sherbok
ISLAM IN A WORLD OF DIVERSE FAITHS (*editor*)
ISSUES IN CONTEMPORARY JUDAISM

Stephen T. Davis
LOGIC AND THE NATURE OF GOD

Clement Dore
MORAL SCEPTICISM
GOD, SUFFERING AND SOLIPSISM

J. Kellenberger
INTER-RELIGIOUS MODELS AND CRITERIA

Adil Özdemir and Kenneth Frank
VISIBLE ISLAM IN MODERN TURKEY

Chakravathi Ram-Prasad
KNOWLEDGE AND LIBERATION IN CLASSICAL INDIAN THOUGHT

Joseph Runzo
IS GOD REAL?

Ninian Smart
BUDDHISM AND CHRISTIANITY

Michael Stoeber
RECLAIMING THEODICY
Reflections on Suffering, Compassion and Spiritual Transformation

Roger Teichmann
ABSTRACT ENTITIES

Donald Wiebe
BEYOND LEGITIMATION

Richard Worsley
HUMAN FREEDOM AND THE LOGIC OF EVIL

Library of Philosophy and Religion
Series Standing Order ISBN 0–333–69996–3
(outside North America only)

You can receive future titles in this series as they are published by placing a standing order. Please contact your bookseller or, in case of difficulty, write to us at the address below with your name and address, the title of the series and the ISBN quoted above.

Customer Service Department, Macmillan Distribution Ltd, Houndmills, Basingstoke, Hampshire RG21 6XS, England

Reclaiming Theodicy

Reflections on Suffering, Compassion and Spiritual Transformation

Michael Stoeber

palgrave
macmillan

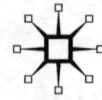

© Michael Stoeber 2005

All rights reserved. No reproduction, copy or transmission of this publication may be made without written permission.

No paragraph of this publication may be reproduced, copied or transmitted save with written permission or in accordance with the provisions of the Copyright, Designs and Patents Act 1988, or under the terms of any licence permitting limited copying issued by the Copyright Licensing Agency, 90 Tottenham Court Road, London W1T 4LP.

Any person who does any unauthorized act in relation to this publication may be liable to criminal prosecution and civil claims for damages.

The author has asserted his right to be identified as the author of this work in accordance with the Copyright, Designs and Patents Act 1988.

First published 2005 by
PALGRAVE MACMILLAN
Houndmills, Basingstoke, Hampshire RG21 6XS and
175 Fifth Avenue, New York, N.Y. 10010
Companies and representatives throughout the world

PALGRAVE MACMILLAN is the global academic imprint of the Palgrave Macmillan division of St. Martin's Press, LLC and of Palgrave Macmillan Ltd. Macmillan® is a registered trademark in the United States, United Kingdom and other countries. Palgrave is a registered trademark in the European Union and other countries.

ISBN-13: 978–1–4039–9762–3
ISBN-10: 1–4039–9762–4

This book is printed on paper suitable for recycling and made from fully managed and sustained forest sources.

A catalogue record for this book is available from the British Library.

Library of Congress Cataloging-in-Publication Data
Stoeber, Michael (Michael F.)
   Reclaiming theodicy : reflections on suffering, compassion, and spiritual transformation / Michael Stoeber.
      p. cm. – (Library of philosophy and religion)
   Includes bibliographical references and index.
   ISBN 1–4039–9762–4
      1. Theodicy. 2. Suffering–Religious aspects–Catholic Church. I. Title.
   II. Library of philosophy and religion (Palgrave (Firm))

BT160.S845 2005
231′.8–dc22   2005048773

10 9 8 7 6 5 4 3 2 1
14 13 12 11 10 09 08 07 06 05

Printed and bound in Great Britain by
Antony Rowe Ltd, Chippenham and Eastbourne

To my teachers, in gratitude

Contents

Preface and Acknowledgements	ix
1 Context and Issues	2
Destructive suffering	2
Spiritual experience	6
Spiritual experience and theodicy	9
2 Transformative Suffering	18
Suffering and spiritual growth	18
Transformative suffering and healing	21
Spiritual transformation, empathy and compassion	26
3 Suffering and Christ	34
Apathy, distorted empathy and compassion	35
Toward a politics of compassion	39
The Passion and Resurrection of Christ	44
The spiritual experience of Christ	47
Christ and spiritual transformation	53
Mystic love and the theodicy question	56
4 Destructive Suffering	60
Destructive suffering and spiritual experience	60
The question of abandoning theodicy	63
The effects of destructive suffering	68
Destructive suffering and afterlife possibilities	72
5 Afterlife Beliefs	80
Suffering and afterlife beliefs	80
Hell and the questions of justice and compassion	83
Heaven and hell	87
Purgatory, rebirth and the hope in universal salvation	91
The hope of theodicy	99
Notes	102
Bibliography	133
Index	140

Preface and Acknowledgements

This book proposes a narrative of life within which one might understand suffering in relation to a personal God of ultimate power and love. It is a reflection on themes of theodicy – theology that defends God in the face of evil. It develops the theme of 'transformative' suffering, showing how some suffering has positive effects on people who struggle with it. The book distinguishes 'destructive suffering,' for which there are no such positive effects, from 'transformative suffering'. It responds to destructive suffering by stressing human and divine compassion and illustrating various spiritual experiences of God that are healing and life-giving. It also proposes possible afterlife contexts that would be appropriate to a religious view which stresses compassion, healing and spiritual growth.

In outline, the spiritual narrative is relatively simple. Certain kinds of suffering contribute positively to transformative growth towards an ideal condition of creative love in spiritual intimacy with God, other human beings, and all of creation. I illustrate this correspondence, describing 'soul-making' theodicy and major issues that are associated with it. I emphasize the nature and role of compassion in such spiritually transformative suffering, as this moral attitude is modelled in the teaching and works of Jesus. In Christianity the life of Jesus provides more than just a pattern of personal and spiritual development for humanity. It also advocates a 'politics' of compassion in response to suffering – of working to institutionalize social structures that are grounded in compassion. Even more significantly, I explore a 'redemptive' dynamic that exists in some Christian spirituality. The suffering, death and Resurrection of Christ reveal for some people both how God is presently open to human suffering and how people in their suffering might come to know and experience God in spiritually intimate ways that are healing, life-giving, and transformative.

Not all suffering is spiritually transformative. Some suffering is bitterly destructive. Because such suffering is pointless and non-redemptive, one must not only labour to protect people from destructive suffering and to help people recover from it, but one must hope for afterlife healing from its experience and for further transformative opportunities in the ongoing movement towards spiritual fulfilment.

Indeed, Christian attitudes of compassion for the victims of extremely destructive suffering demand this hope in afterlife possibilities. This is not to suggest that destructive suffering comes to serve some positively transformative purpose for the victim of it (and hence is not really evil after all), but rather it is to express the hope that such non-redemptive suffering does not finally defeat the spiritual ideal. It is to hope for appropriate contexts of healing and recovery from destructive suffering, and for further opportunities for spiritual growth and transformation, despite the harsh reality of destructive suffering. So, rather than abandoning theodicy in the face of destructive suffering, as some contemporary theologians advocate, I propose speculative outlines of purgatory, rebirth, hell, heaven and universal salvation. These afterlife possibilities follow consistently from my reflections on transformative and destructive suffering, and are related to the social and communal context of healing and hope in this world.

The book is developed in creative and constructive dialogue with a wide variety of theologians and philosophers, but especially with Fyodor Dostoevsky, Louis Dupré, John Hick and Dorothee Soelle. It is ecumenical and even somewhat inter-religious in orientation, though framed within my own Catholic Christian background and experience. I have attempted to make the book accessible to a non-academic audience while at the same time maintaining an intellectual rigour which is sensitive to current academic issues pertaining to the religious problem of suffering. So specialized, technical language has been minimized as much as possible in the text-body itself and discussion of relevant scholarly debates in theodicy have been largely restricted to the endnotes, which in some cases are quite long and detailed. The arguments respond to two types of critic: to sceptics of religion who in their condemnation of Christian approaches to suffering neglect elements of spiritual experience that are crucial to effective theodicy, both at a practical–pastoral and a theoretical level; and to those contemporary Christian theologians who advocate the abandonment of theodicy altogether as a theological enterprise – of all attempts to defend the Christian God against the harsh realities of suffering. This latter position appears to be becoming quite popular, given current anti-foundationalist tendencies within various circles of academia. So the book is a reclaiming of the legitimacy and significance of theodicy, or at least the beginning of such a reclamation.

In many ways this little book is very close to my heart. It marks a lot of positive change for me. I feel grateful to Dan Bunyard, John Hick and Palgrave Macmillan for publishing it and to the folks who supported me and my family during the difficult period in which much of it was written, including my colleagues at Regis College and St Clement's, and especially certain friends: Rafael Indart, Dana Kasprzyk, Rochelle Martin, Chris McDonald, Ricardo Oliva, L. B. Raschka, Gord Stevenson, Claudio Valdez and Roger Yaworski.

A number of people generously provided constructive criticism of the book. Their assistance does not mean that they agree with all my views or arguments nor, of course, are they responsible for the limitations and deficiencies of the book. Most notably, in responding to the whole of the book, Don Evans provided important advice and encouragement. Paul Gooch and Ovey Mohammed stimulated quite helpful organizational changes and additions at the later stages of writing. My sincere thanks go out also to those who helped on various specific chapters: Bill Barbieri, Jr, Peter Casarella, Rod Cardamone, Stephanie Ford, Dan Kuntz, Rosemary MacDonald, Ron Mercier, Terry Penelhum, Michael Vertin and Bill Whitesell.

As journal editors, Michael Jordan and Bill Arnal supported me in the publication of two chapters of the manuscript and have given me permission to draw on them here: 'Hell, Divine Love, and Divine Justice', *Logos*, Vol. 2 (1999), 176–99, and 'Transformative Suffering, Destructive Suffering, and the Question of Abandoning Theodicy', *Studies in Religion*, Vol. 32 (2003), 429–47. An early version of Chapter 5 was presented at the workshop, 'Religion and Torture', sponsored by the Program of Medieval Studies, Rutgers University, April 1996. My appreciation goes out to Karl Morrison for the invitation to participate in that event and his gracious hospitality.

I appreciate also Vanessa Mitchell's careful reading of the typescript as well as the editorial support of Dorothy Cummings and her help in refining the title of the book. My thanks also to administration at Regis College – J.A. Loftus, Joe Schner and Ron Mercier – for providing both the resources for Dorothy's help and the generous research time for the book.

Finally, I need to thank especially my children, Anne and Tom, and my wife, Lois, for their patience and confidence in me.

All quotes from the Bible come from *The New American Bible: with Revised New Testament and Revised Psalms* (Nashville: Catholic Bible Press, 1987). I have tried to use inclusive language throughout my text, but I have for the most part left the exclusive references given in quotations from other sources.

The ink sketches on the cover and at the beginning of the chapters were done by me, during the time I was writing the book. The sketch on the book jacket is 'Winter Solstice', Silver Spring, Maryland, 1994.

Easter Monday 2005

M.F.S.
Regis College
Toronto School of Theology
University of Toronto

'Tree of Life'
Toronto, 2003

1
Context and Issues

> From noon onward, darkness came over the whole land until three in the afternoon. And about three o'clock Jesus cried out in a loud voice, *'Eli, Eli, lema sabachthani?'*, which means, 'My God, my God, why have you forsaken me?'
>
> Matthew 27: 45–6

Destructive suffering

The inspiration for this book comes from a close friend who shared with me an extremely painful event she experienced. We had been helping each other in various ways over a long period of time and had come together again in a meditation group that was open to emotional–spiritual work. In the dynamic of this setting my friend recalled previously repressed childhood memories. Although I have heard other disturbing accounts given by both victims and even some victimizers of childhood trauma, this particular incident was most shocking. In this instance my friend *relived* the terror of a childhood experience in a setting where the group was deeply connected at various emotional and spiritual levels. I am convinced that the group provided deep empathetic stimulus and support that was essential to her particular awakening to her past horrors. Compassion, a major theme of this book, provided the context necessary to initiate the healing process. And though some of us knew she was ripe for some process, none of us quite expected her story, not even she herself. As a young child she was brutally attacked by someone whom she knew and trusted.

Later, my friend spoke to me about how she was beginning to understand the source of her anger and resentment towards God in terms of this particular trauma. She spoke hopefully about how perhaps she could begin to be more open to the spiritual presence of Christ. I was taken aback by this remark because she is open in prayer and meditation to spirit and noted for her compassionate warmth and wonderful healing touch. I knew she was of Catholic background and so had assumed all along that she had the same openness to Christ she exhibited towards various spiritual presences and energies. We went on to talk about our struggles, about the traumatic suffering we and others had experienced as children, about the pain we are working to overcome. She asked me how God could allow such horrors to be inflicted upon children. Indeed, how could one be open to a God who permitted such atrocities?

Since she knew I had written a book on God and the problem of evil, my friend expected helpful answers. Putting on my professor's hat, I moved into my head, and began to respond in abstract terms of spiritual transformation, how we can learn by and through our suffering, how suffering can be conducive to emotional and spiritual growth. But the shock from my intimate psychic connection to my friend's childhood horror quickly brought me back into my body. I began to stumble and stutter, realizing as I was speaking that I was dangerously close to denying the evil that was done to her as a child, suggesting that it might be somehow good for her, that she would become 'better' through its overcoming, that perhaps, for example, she would now be able to help heal people who had undergone similar horrors.

There is some truth to these views, I think. Some very traumatic suffering can nevertheless be positively transformative or at least contribute to some good effect. But I had also felt deeply her experience as a child, helpless, brutally victimized. Her suffering in this case seemed utterly destructive. There was nothing good about this particular experience, no transformative context for it whatsoever. To say there was would fly in the face of the horror I experienced with her, and move me away from the loving empathy I was presently feeling for her.[1] Moreover, I soon realized that it was possible that my friend might still not overcome this particular trauma. There was still much extremely painful processing to be done with it. It came very close to destroying her own spirit and might still overwhelm her, just as childhood traumas have indiscriminately destroyed so many other people.

Indeed, these are the terms of Ivan Karamazov's rebellion in Fyodor Dostoevsky's famous novel, *The Brothers Karamazov*. Ivan will have nothing to do with God's purposes of creation simply because of the suffering perpetrated upon helpless and innocent children. Apart from the incredible horror and pain that are forced upon some children, there is the harsh fact that not all of them do or ever will recover in this lifetime from the brutalities that are inflicted upon them. The reason why Ivan's rebellion is so profound and influential is because it arises out of *love* (though in Ivan's case much distortion of this love eventually emerges in the story), and this love is focused upon innocent children. He turns the very essence of the Christian God, LOVE, against God. How can Ivan accept the Christian God and His/Her world while at the same time respecting and loving those children who are tortured in it? If Ivan accepts God and God's world and purposes, he would be saying the suffering of the children is OK, we need not worry overly much about it, that it somehow fits into the cosmic scheme – that it is somehow not as bad as it seems. But this only taints or diminishes the love Ivan feels towards these children. He will not give up his compassionate outrage at their plight. After all, if God can somehow magically transform their suffering into good in the context of an afterlife miracle, then it isn't such a big deal after all. But to Ivan their suffering is most significant. He is deeply and genuinely compassionate. And his moral anger forces him to have nothing to do with this Christian God and His providence, simply out of his love for these poor, innocent children. This is the 'theodicy' question for Ivan: how, indeed, can one be respectfully open to an all-powerful Being who creates the conditions of such brutality and oversees these horrors?

Ivan asks his younger brother Alyosha: ' "Tell me yourself, I challenge you – answer. Imagine that you are creating a fabric of human destiny with the object of making men happy in the end, giving them peace and rest at last, but that it was essential and inevitable to torture to death only one tiny creature – that little child beating its breast with its fist, for instance – and to found that edifice on its unavenged tears, would you consent to be the architect on those conditions? Tell me, and tell the truth." '[2] Alyosha, the young mystic, the aspiring monk, replies no, he would not. He too loves children. Indeed, it is this particular aspect of the problem of evil which moves some Christians today to abandon their faith completely. I suspect it moves others away from the idea of a loving and creative divine Being who actively participates in Her/His creation, towards some more impersonal and monistic conceptions that are given in westernized versions of certain eastern religions. For in these non-theistic religious views this question of God's relation to the brutality in this world does not obtain because ultimate Reality is not conceived as personal, creative and as lovingly oriented towards the world.

Ivan's rebellion leaves Alyosha disturbed and shaken, to the point of confessing to Ivan that he himself could not admit the creation of a world which is founded on the unexpiated blood of even one of the innocent victims Ivan describes. Ivan's account is simple and vivid, focusing on the suffering of children, but it extends to all people who have experienced extremely destructive suffering, like my friend who inspired this book. Moreover, his passionate account reflects brutalities which extend well beyond his nineteenth-century illustrations. Alyosha's response to Ivan, that he too could not institute or endorse a system which involves the unredeemed suffering and deaths of innocent victims, is sincere and forthright, confirming his honourable character. But he adds to this confession an intriguing qualification which seems out of sorts with his initial moral frankness: ' "Brother," said Alyosha suddenly, with flashing eyes, "you said just now, is there a being in the whole world who would have the right to forgive and could forgive? But there is a Being and He can forgive everything, all *and for all*, because He gave His innocent blood for all and everything. You have forgotten Him, and on Him is built the edifice, and it is to Him they cry aloud, "Thou art just, O Lord, for thy ways are revealed!" '[3]

Given the context, Alyosha's allusion to Jesus seems forced and impulsive, not wholly consistent with his concern about the moral status of creation in light of its many unredeemed horrors. How does this reference to Jesus help me or my friend respond to her destructive suffering? What does *forgiveness* have to do with the issue in question, the poor innocent victims of such vicious brutalities? And how does Christ's death secure justice? Surely Alyosha is not suggesting the ransom to the devil has been duly paid, or that somehow the Divine–human sacrifice brings appropriate satisfaction to the cosmic injustice of original sin, and so justifies the children's experience of destructive suffering. How, indeed, are the divine purposes *in relation to the suffering children revealed in the crucifixion of Jesus?*

Ivan himself anticipates Alyosha's reference: ' "Ah! the One without sin and His blood! No, I have not forgotten Him; on the contrary I've been wondering all the time how it was you did not bring Him in before, for usually all arguments on your side put him in the foreground." '[4] However, Ivan does not expand upon this tendency of theologians to refer to the significance of the suffering, death and Resurrection of Jesus in response to utterly destructive human suffering. Rather, he goes on in his story of the Grand Inquisitor to develop the difficulties of freedom in the context of the spiritual vision and ideal of Christianity. And Alyosha, despite his own initial move towards Jesus, also remains silent about the importance of Christ in relation to the atrocities witnessed by Ivan in his rebellion. He never explicitly expands on the significance of Jesus in responding to the realities of evil, although his compassionate attitudes and actions in the story have been interpreted by some readers as illustrating the appropriate practical response to the problem.[5] Indeed, traditionally the Christian redemption in Jesus is perceived more as a mystery of faith rather than a tool for philosophy. As Louis Dupré puts it, 'True enough, on the cross philosophy suffers shipwreck, believers and unbelievers unanimously declare.'[6]

However, it seems to me that the spiritual reality of Christ to which Alyosha is pointing in his response to Ivan does have significance for 'theodicy', by which I mean here theological themes that defend the power and love of God in responding to the problem of evil. Reference to the suffering, death and Resurrection of Jesus help especially to defend divine goodness and love in a practical way, showing its role as a positive medium in the response to the problem of pain and suffering. The Passion and Resurrection of Jesus illustrate divine goodness for those who *participate* in various degrees in Christ's 'redemptive' event. I will explore the nature of this healing and life-giving dynamic throughout this book. From some Christian perspectives it becomes a key in understanding the nature of suffering, and even a lever in the transformation of evil into good. As I will discuss in Chapter 3, it is the paramount example for Christians of the divine presence *in creation*, one that brings a perspective to suffering within which a human being can understand his/her own life. But, more important, in responding to victims of extremely destructive suffering, it points to the possibility of actually drawing the Divine and the Divine's healing power into their life and world, through intimate, personal spiritual experience.

Spiritual experience

Today, in our 'post-modern' world, spiritual experience is often regarded merely as a subjective phenomenon, as the way in which certain people interpret and integrate their world religiously. It is typically thought not to involve an actual contact or intimate connection between humanity and the divine Presence or spiritual realities. God is in this view considered to be presently inaccessible. God is the transcendent and ineffable Mystery, and so regarded as wholly beyond human language, feeling, and thought. Positive descriptions of the Divine (for example, as 'loving', 'compassionate', and 'just') are thought to be human interpretations of the divine Mystery. They are conceptions which are helpful to subjective, human religious experience but not properly applicable to the enigmatic wholly Other, who transcends completely these symbolic references.

Traditionally, Christian theologians proposed the theory of analogical language in order to secure the meaningfulness of our language about God. When we ascribe descriptive characteristics to God, we of course cannot mean these univocally, in exactly the same sense as we would mean when we used that language in normal contexts, given the transcendent and superlative nature of the divine Being. On the other hand, if our language about God is to have any significance at all, it cannot be equivocal, of completely different meaning from that same language given in reference to finite objects of this world. So theologians proposed that our reference to God must have analogical meaning. There must be a way in which God truly reflects how we describe Him or Her, even if it is only proportionally and the described property is present in different ways with respect to God. So in this view God's love, compassion and justice are both like and unlike human love, compassion and justice. Although these are human ideas (symbols) about God, they are thought to have some meaningful referents *in* God, even though they are not wholly equivalent in meaning to our normal connotations of love, compassion and justice.

However, for many contemporary theologians, language about God has only subjective connotations. Many religious people today presume that such properties *in* God are wholly inaccessible to us given God's utter transcendence. They speak of experiencing God, but this experience is a matter of interpreting and integrating one's life in terms of religious symbols and ideals. All human experience is contextualized according to human categories of interpretation. God 'lives' or is 'actualized' only in human ideas (for example, of love, compassion, and justice), and the experience of God is thought to be a particular way of *human* being-in-the-world.[7] In these views, spiritual experience becomes a wholly subjective phenomenon, excluding the possibility of God or spiritual realities contributing anything directly or immediately to it.

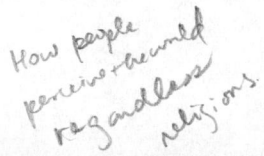

This seems to me to assume a very narrow view of what spiritual experience might involve. If one regards spiritual experience solely in terms of human attitudes, feelings and thoughts, then the difference between religious believers and atheistic sceptics becomes simply a matter of how they interpret their experiences of the world – whether they perceive the world religiously or not – rather than a matter of any real encounter (or none) with the divine Reality. More important, if one excludes at the outset the possibility in religious experience of influences beyond that of subjective human emotions and imagination, then one narrowly delimits experiential possibilities. Such views actually inhibit the experience of God as Reality, distinct from and positively influencing human feelings and thoughts.

It is true that spiritual experience normally has a context by which we interpret and understand the experience. In most religious experiences one inevitably brings concepts, ideas and feelings both to the spiritual encounter and to the subsequent meaning that is given to the encounter, just as one does in normal encounters with empirical, phenomenal things. But one must be careful in seeking to understand religious experience not to rule out at the start the very possibility of an actual point of contact with realities distinct from oneself. Religious experience is in part dependent on human expectations and is very much inhibited by human resistances. One must be open in prayer or meditation or ritual worship to spiritual realities that exist quite apart and distinct from human feelings and images in order to become aware of their presence and influence, be they discarnate saints or people, angels, or various modes or forms of God. These realities are non-physical, but if one becomes open to them one can begin to feel their actual presence or energies through the body, emotions or our various spiritual intuitions.

I am not suggesting here that all reports of spiritual awareness or encounters ought to be uncritically accepted as genuine experiences of spiritual reality. Indeed, as with all human experience, psychological distortion and fantasy affect past and contemporary spiritualities. Moreover, subjective unconscious material plays a significant part in spiritual life and can influence one's spiritual growth in both negative and positive ways. It is crucial that one critically reflect upon one's own spiritual experiences and evaluate carefully claims about such encounters that are made by others. But I would insist that some human experience does coincide with authentic spiritual realities, quite apart from the strictly subjective contents of one's personal and collective unconscious. In particular, I would contend that many people do encounter intimately the real spiritual presence of Christ. The history of Christian spirituality, especially of Christian mysticism, bears immense support for this view.

This point about the nature of spiritual experience is especially important to this book. In our contemporary western culture there is a general resistance to the possibility of intimate awareness and union with spiritual realities. Modern and post-modern worldviews have tended in their materialistic emphases even to presume the non-existence of spiritual realities. This in turn inhibits the promise of profound healing that a person in the midst of suffering might receive through opening to such contact. The spiritual perspective I am proposing here claims that the Divine–human encounter is one wherein the human subject becomes affectively touched and influenced by, and sometimes aware of, various facets of God or different spiritual realities. Spiritual experience, in this view, is not just a matter of interpreting everyday experiences in terms of ideas about God, but rather one of incorporating and integrating one's actual encounters with God and spiritual realities into everyday life.[8] So, in this view of spirituality, which I will define more carefully in Chapter 2, religious experience can profoundly affect one's approach and response to suffering.[9]

Spiritual experience and theodicy

Indeed, an overriding question of this book is the character and function of this more spiritual understanding of God in relation to the Christian treatment of suffering. How does the spiritual experience of God affect one's perception and experience of suffering? What is the power and significance such a stance possesses in responding to the problem of evil?

To begin to explore these questions I clarify different approaches to suffering, especially in relation to the suffering of other people. But the focus in Chapter 2 is on suffering which leads to and arises in compassion. This is vital to the particular spiritual understanding of God that I develop. The concern is the nature of the experience and transformation of suffering in the development and expression of human compassion. Certain suffering is understood in relation to a purpose or goal of human creation and life, one which is grounded in a compassionate God and within which some suffering is thought to contribute positively to the moral and spiritual transformation of self and others.

Of course, not all suffering can be interpreted in such a positive fashion. One need only to glance at the newspaper to be reminded how the world in which we live can be so very destructive. I have remarked earlier about the destructive suffering of my friend. In light of such horrors, religious sceptics mockingly declare that God must have been jesting when He pronounces in the book of *Genesis* the world to be good. How do we make sense of the immense suffering of the world if God is all-good, all-powerful and all-knowing? Why does God not intervene in this state of affairs, to reduce or even eliminate the immense destructive suffering humanity and other creatures must bear? Why does God permit such pervasive suffering? These are the kinds of simple questions of theodicy that my friend posed to me in response to her own destructive affliction.

A very popular and powerful response to these questions is that of freewill. Clearly, much if not most of the suffering of the world is a direct consequence of human action.[10] Moral evil, then, is explained in reference to human freedom, which God has given us and permits us to play out. But this raises questions surrounding the rationale and the negative effects of such freedom. Fyodor Dostoevsky voices the main issue in *The Brothers Karamazov*: it appears to make a mockery of humanity, because we obviously fail so miserably to fulfil our potential as moral beings. We spend so much of our freetime hurting others and ourselves. Freedom in the knowledge of good and evil leads to tremendous destructive suffering. Yet Jewish and Christian mythology tells us that human suffering is integral to this freedom in the knowledge of good and evil. In the myth of the Fall, Adam and Eve are banished from the Garden of Eden after they eat the fruit of the tree of moral knowledge. Thereafter, they are subject to the suffering of this world. But the myth also suggests the possible significance of freewill for the question of human suffering. In it, Eve is told that the knowledge of good and evil – moral knowledge in freedom – is the means whereby we can 'be like gods'. Remarkably, God confirms this truth later in the story: 'Then the Lord God said: 'See! [They have] become like one of us, knowing what is good and what is bad!' (*Genesis* 3: 5, 22)

So there is clearly a way in which Eve's disobedience can be understood to be a good thing, a very good thing indeed, despite the fact that it also involves the terrible loss of some primitive intimacy with God and with others. I think it is important that positive spins on the Fall myth never lose sight of the terrible tragedy of the human condition, the radical self-isolation from God and others that freewill in spiritual growth involves, and the immense amount of suffering that such a separation and independence entails. Nevertheless, in focusing so on the harshness of life it is important also not to ignore the positive intimations in the story. It is a powerful myth that provocatively marks for us the dawning of moral consciousness and freedom, in the history of human transformation towards its spiritual fulfilment.[11]

This freedom in the knowledge of good and evil will not be regarded as a good thing by people who would rather spend their time in the safety and comfort of some opulent and tranquil paradise. That is perhaps the kind of vision some critics have in mind when they ask why our happiness must be dependent upon our suffering first. But if one is looking for opportunities by which to learn, problems to tackle, and situations which challenge all aspects of ourselves, then this world might very well be an appropriate environment. Despite its incredible horrors, which at times can simply overwhelm us in their depth and intensity, there is much beauty and good in our world, and much more to be had in our present and future struggles. We are pushed, sometimes to our limits, and we learn and grow and love in and through and by our suffering.

This idea of transformative suffering is the topic especially of Chapters 2 and 3. I think most people, if they really thought about it, would have it no other way. They would rather embrace with love and exuberance Eve's initial longing to become like God than be pampered in an eternal state of child-like innocence without moral responsibility and human dignity. They would choose what John Hick calls this 'soul-making' journey,[12] even if it means that not all of their suffering-experiences will be positive or lead to spiritual growth. Chapter 5 suggests that in this spiritual perspective we are not here to be rewarded with heaven through obedient behaviour. We are here to become heavenly beings. This requires that we be moral beings.

This majestic religious ideal requires a wide-ranging freedom in the knowledge of good and evil. The divine-likeness is not something God can actualize simply by the snap of His/Her fingers. It requires human choice, will and cooperation towards such development, which means that people can choose against their spiritual potential. Indeed, this freedom means people can choose to do incredibly cruel things to others, including acts which tragically remove the victims from this very environment which is supposedly created specially for their spiritual development.

However, perhaps we should not presume that spiritual development ends in this lifetime. Indeed, death, like birth, is a great mystery. Surely an all-powerful God can create future life-conditions within which human beings might find their healing from destructive suffering and continue to aspire towards their spiritual fulfilment? This would not take away the terrible experiences of evil that all of us have to endure at various times in our lives. But it would ensure the possibility of some appropriate healing context and the continued journey towards the spiritual ideal for those victims who in this life are so tragically consumed by their suffering.

In a religious context, as we will see in Chapters 4 and 5, authentic compassion for these victims would seem to require such afterlife possibilities. But compassion also brings into question the appropriateness of this world as an environment for spiritual development. Even those of us who would choose moral responsibility and dignity over a childlike innocence in paradise would rather have a world where there was much less tragedy and moral evil. Even if we should expect some destructive evil and suffering in a 'soul-making' world, maybe God could place certain limitations on our freedom and intervene more often and directly in the world so as to reduce the extent and severity of destructive suffering. Perhaps also there could be far less natural evil in our world. In that regard, Terence Penelhum observes the very negative 'implications of evolutionary biology' – the way in which 'the creative process itself has involved massive extinctions and forms of suffering that have not been perpetrated by free creatures'.[13]

For example, as I am preparing this manuscript for publication authorities are still responding to the Indian Ocean tsunami of 26 December, 2004. This immense disaster painfully reminds us of the precarious nature of life on earth. Rescue workers responded in huge numbers, as massive relief-support efforts have been organized locally here in Toronto and throughout the world. But there are estimates of between 160,000 and 230,000 deaths, and many more injured, orphaned and homeless. These numbers are simply staggering and numbing. The horror is accentuated by the fact that we now possess the technological knowledge and skill to reduce significantly through preventive measures the heavy loss of human life associated with this kind of natural disaster. In this case, the affected areas of the tsunami did not have the warning devices that are already in place in areas of the Pacific Ocean. Indeed, we now have the economic, agricultural, medical and technical resources to eliminate a tremendous amount of the suffering that arises worldwide in the context of various 'natural' evils. Yet often we lack the social-cooperative will to do so.

How are we to respond theologically in the face of such immense, natural destruction as the Indian Ocean tsunami of 2004? If we suppose a God of infinite power and love, we must presume there to be afterlife conditions sufficient for the healing and continued spiritual growth of these victims of such destructive suffering. I think this point is being neglected in many current discussions of theodicy. I will argue in Chapter 4 that it is a minimum requirement of theology. However, it does seem possible that a journey which moves us towards the likeness of God might be realized under conditions where there is less destructive evil and suffering in this world. Then again, maybe the ideal cannot be achieved under less severe conditions. Perhaps this world is the only way. The great depth and scope of evil in our world can lead one to wonder about these questions. But as a Christian, the spiritual point of life seems clear to me: to become like Christ – to aspire towards the likeness of God – to struggle to be open to the graced movement towards this ideal.

This spiritual narrative I am proposing here might sound simplistic and a bit too optimistic and preachy. But the details of this brief sketch will begin to be filled out in this book in reference to the work of a wide variety of insightful theologians and philosophers. It seems to me a much more compelling religious view of the world and of God than contemporary 'deistic' versions that are currently popular. 'Deism' is a religious view which supposes a radical distance, separation and even relative independence between God and the created world. For example, in a 1998 editorial in the *New Republic*, James Wood criticizes western, theistic religions for depicting the world as rather like a laboratory of God, wherein He can observe human obedience to the first two commandments, 'Love thy God, and love thy neighbour.' Mr Wood asks why, under these conditions, human freewill should be 'important for God'? He mockingly imagines in his speculations that this lab is overseen by a distant and detached God, One who 'watches us drown in our own incomprehension' of the horrors of so much destructive suffering.[14]

If it were not for the current popularity of such a naive version of theistic religious visions, one would be surprised and perhaps even shocked by it being voiced by a university-educated editor of such a reputedly 'intellectual' and respected magazine. Certainly that is not the kind of God Who is envisioned and encountered in the Christian religious perspective espoused in this book. William Blake insists: 'Think not thou canst sigh a sigh/And thy maker is not by;/Think not thou canst weep a tear/And thy maker is not near.'[15] The God Who most Christians aspire towards is not the deistic despot that sceptics such as Mr Wood have in mind. Rather, in the view adopted here, God knows our suffering intimately and we can come to experience God *in* this infinite compassion. Indeed, that is what it means, in large part, to become 'Christ-like'. As I will illustrate in Chapter 3, this requires a contemplative opening of one's heart and consciousness to a passionate God who tenderly underlies and permeates this world. This God, a God of Love, is one who positively thrives on intimate relationships. And life is not a laboratory of testing within a cosmic moral scheme geared towards a future reward or punishment according to the strict measure of one's obedience and disobedience to moral law. Rather, life is envisioned as an environment of human moral and spiritual transformation (or regression), oriented towards a future divine life of creative love in spiritual intimacy with God, humanity and all of creation.

These religious views – of God, of the divine purpose of life, and of the human experience of God and spiritual realities – differ significantly from those ideas with which critics such as James Wood take issue. The barbs of those sceptics are directed at an apathetic straw-God and they picture humanity as lacking integrity, purpose, and the possibility of relationship with their heartless keeper. It is not so much that the critics miss the mark, but that they are aiming at the wrong target. In contrast, in a Christian spiritual context – what Louis Dupré calls 'Concrete-Religious' conceptions – the Divine is immanent in a world where humanity exists in dignified progress towards a divine life. In such views, the life of Christ becomes crucial in understanding the nature and purpose of suffering and the human response to it.

In this book I focus on particular spiritual views and experiences of Christ, where his suffering, death and Resurrection are understood as playing a significant role in the moral and spiritual transformation that might occur through one's own painful transformative dynamic. The experience of Christ, which can occur at various levels of awareness, has a positive bearing on issues in theodicy in that it illustrates how the Divine is both open to human suffering and positively affects those people who participate in various degrees in this ongoing redemptive event. As I show in Chapter 3, this spiritual dynamic provides deep consolation for our suffering. Moreover, it also grounds and charges the image of the transformative ideal, one that is actually evidenced in the experiences and consequent orientations of many ordinary people, but most strikingly and consistently in the lifestyles of some special exemplars of the ideal – those to whom I refer to in this book as 'mystic-saints'. Nevertheless, all Christians are called to respond to suffering compassionately and to work towards developing a 'politics' of compassion which might transform institutional structures in positive ways and greatly reduce destructive suffering.

Illustrating this spiritual framework of theodicy requires a conceptual analysis of some of the basic attitudes involved in the transformative dynamic. So I explore in Chapter 3 'apathy' and various forms of 'passion' – including compassionate empathy and empathy in its distorted forms of sadism and masochism – and relate these attitudes to the idea of spiritual transformation. Moreover, in Chapter 5 I extend both this analysis of fundamental human passions and the view of spiritual transformation to the question of various afterlife possibilities. Ideas of distorted passions, compassion and spiritual transformation provide the basis for a critical evaluation of different views of purgatory, heaven, hell, universal salvation and reincarnation.

In light of this spiritual narrative I also examine in Chapter 4 the problem of destructive suffering. This is suffering that serves no positive purpose. It is wholly negative suffering which can even hinder quite radically one's spiritual growth. Although I cautiously suggest that some destructive suffering can play a positive role in the spiritual transformation of people who observe and respond compassionately to its effects, I acknowledge and illustrate how it remains tragically and utterly non-transformative for the victims. This is the greatest obstacle to belief in the spiritually transformative role of suffering. Despite the consolation and power of spiritual experience in the transformation of some suffering, the religious purposes of life seem to be defeated by utterly destructive suffering. In response to this concern, I argue in Chapters 4 and 5 that the theme of transformative suffering requires the postulation of some continuation of this spiritual process, possibly in the context of a realm of purgatory or by returning, through rebirth, to this environment. Such afterlife speculation answers hopefully and compassionately to those who are consumed by their destructive suffering in this life.

But I begin in Chapter 2 with some observations about the relevance of suffering to human growth and development. Suffering is crucial to certain views of physical, intellectual and moral development, and is essential also to the idea of spiritual integration and transformation.

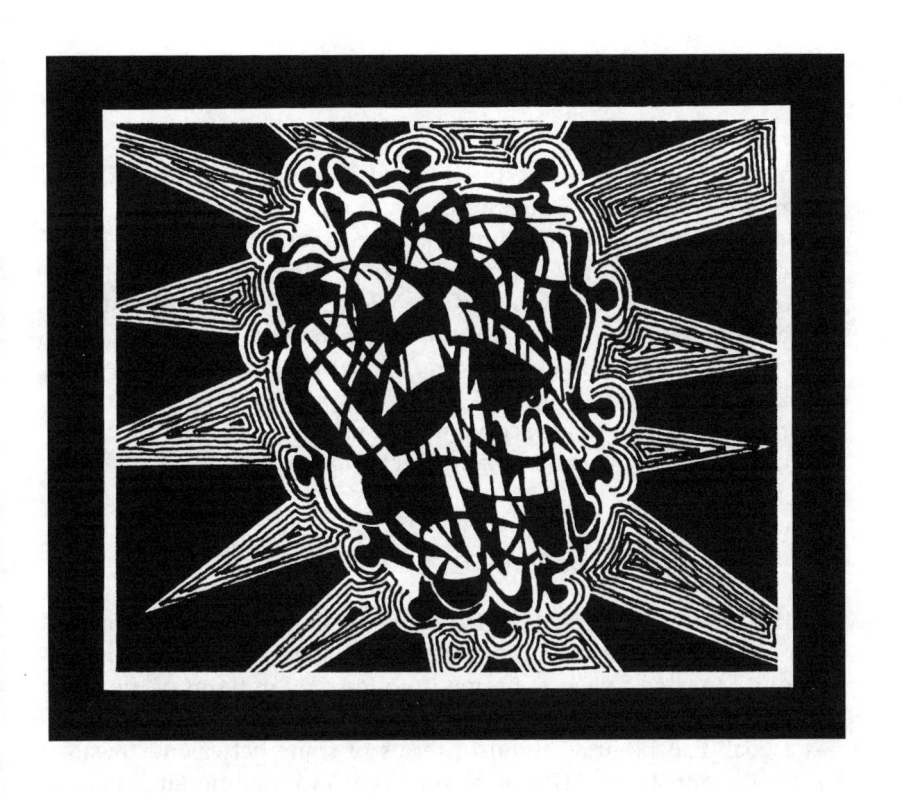

'Sacred Circle'
Toronto, 1997

2
Transformative Suffering

> After he had taken them [his family] across the stream and had brought over all his possessions, Jacob was left there alone. Then some man wrestled with him until the break of dawn. When the man saw that he could not prevail over him, he struck Jacob's hip at its socket, so that the hip socket was wrenched as they wrestled. The man then said, 'Let me go, for it is daybreak.' But Jacob said, 'I will not let you go until you bless me.' 'What is your name?' the man asked. He answered, 'Jacob.' Then the man said, 'You shall no longer be spoken of as Jacob, but as Israel, because you have contended with divine and human beings and have prevailed.'
>
> *Genesis* 32: 24–9

Suffering and spiritual growth

Writing in a very general way, Dorothee Soelle argues that humanity 'learns through suffering ..., experiences change, is directed towards wisdom'.[1] In such a view, suffering is understood in terms of the positive role it might play in one's life. That is to say, it serves a purpose, has a goal, can be understood in terms of some better end towards which it contributes. This is a very old and traditional religious response to the problem of suffering. We find it, for example, in *The Letter to the Hebrews*, where the writer admonishes his audience to remember and honour the suffering that Jesus endured for humanity. They are told to regard their own trials as a moral training and spiritual discipline that is lovingly permitted by God for their sake:

> Endure your trials as 'discipline'; God treats you as children. For what 'child' is there whose parent does not discipline? ... [Our

earthly parents] disciplined us for a short time as seemed right to them, but God does so for our benefit, in order that we might share his holiness.

At the time, all discipline seems a cause not for joy but for pain, yet later it brings the peaceful fruit of righteousness to those who are trained by it.

So strengthen your drooping hands and your weak knees. Make straight paths for your feet, that what is lame may not be dislocated but healed. (*Hebrews* 12: 7–13)[2]

The writer urges the community to be open to healing and suggests that their suffering might be positively transformative, leading them towards conditions of righteousness and holiness. It is a feature of moral learning and spiritual growth, and so considered to be constructive and purposeful. Certainly, not all suffering can be construed in such a positive fashion. In Chapter 4 I will explore the nature and significance of destructive suffering – suffering which is purposeless and even inhibiting of any kind of personal growth. But in this chapter I will focus on suffering which has creatively beneficial consequences. We are all familiar with the good that can arise through various kinds of suffering. Athletes, for example, attest to the harsh physical pain of training that is necessary to bring out their best performances. But there is also much emotional pain associated with the sacrifices and the intensity of high-level competition – the agonies of defeat, the fears of failure, and other various anxieties that surface in an athlete's struggle to achieve or maintain her or his peak performance.

The same dynamic applies to other disciplines and fields of endeavour. Although intellectual work does not normally include the manner or degree of physical pain involved in physical athletics, it too can involve much suffering. It requires a discipline and perseverance which does not come easily to many of us, and includes various kinds of emotional pain, depending upon the person's abilities, disposition and history. However, one learns in the process, advancing oneself in various ways, opening up new horizons, expanding one's skills and consciousness, and progressing steadily in a gradual unfolding of one's creative and critical potentials. To complete a book, for example, a good book at any rate, normally involves much anguish and frustration along the way. So too in the fine arts, there are struggles preceding the satisfying joy of accomplishment and there are emotional pains closely associated with the expansive skills, insights, and gifts of creation that one hopes to share finally with others.[3] Certainly, not all suffering that is associated with artistic and intellectual accomplishments has a personally transformative effect for the artist or author, even if the product inspires and enriches others in that way. However, much suffering *is* correlative to the growth dynamic by which we become better people and crucial to the movement towards our fulfilment. It is through suffering, at least in part, that we activate and realize our hidden strengths and potentials, be they physical, intellectual or aesthetic.

Suffering can be triggered by an extremely wide range of phenomena and contexts, depending upon an individual's dispositions, attitudes, hopes, desires, expectations, fears and situations. For example, to describe only a few of the extremes within which suffering might arise: from conditions of powerlessness or from guilty feelings over the abuse of power; from constrictions of an extremely limited freedom or from unsettled indecisiveness within a very expansive autonomy; and from radical social isolation or from lack of personal privacy.[4] It all depends on the person's personal characteristics, circumstances, potentials and abilities. More generally, it is clear that suffering is sometimes triggered by and closely associated with the neurological sensation of pain. However, it is a mental state distinct from physical pain. John Hick defines it as 'that state of mind in which we wish violently or obsessively that our situation were otherwise. Such a state of mind involves memory and anticipation, the capacity to imagine alternatives, and (in [humanity]) a moral conscience.'[5]

Suffering, then, is the experience of emotional pain – a mode of consciousness that can arise directly from the sensation of intense physical pain, but which need not at all be associated with it. Suffering is a painful state of consciousness that we wish we did not have to experience. However, often, in struggling through the situation which induces such suffering, we overcome it and transmute it, and grow in various respects: we gain skills and knowledge, we become more aware of life's gifts and pleasures, we become more resilient to life's conflicts, or we acquire a depth of moral character not otherwise possible. Suffering can stimulate the search for life-enriching meaning, or it can lead to the development of facets of one's personality or character that make one a better or more complete person, or it can awaken one to such beneficial qualities. So suffering is linked closely with physical, intellectual, and moral growth.

Suffering can be related to the idea of spiritual growth in the same way. By 'spirituality' I mean most generally a seeking to overcome a deep self-isolating orientation, what some modern writers term a fundamental narcissistic standpoint. This fundamental narcissistic stance inhibits or even distorts one's relationship to God, other human beings, and the created world, as well as one's ability to grow spiritually through these relationships. Spiritual growth occurs through the transformation and integration of various emotional, intellectual, and moral facets of one's self and life. The source and foci of such positive change are a personal, spiritual Source and various spiritual realities. In this view, the Divine grounds yet transcends the individual person and the phenomenal world. Spiritual transformation involves one in an increasingly more intimate connection with God, other people and creation.[6]

John Hick helpfully draws this sense of spirituality into relationship with moral development, and he begins to express it in Christian terms that have a general ecumenical application. He writes:

> The central work of moral and spiritual growth is the overcoming of egoity, the transcending of individual self-interest in a common human life in relation to God. As the essence of all sin is selfishness, so its opposite is a negating of the self-regarding ego. Growth in this 'self-naughting', or liberation from the ego, shows itself in the growth of that love for others which is the essence of morality. To overcome natural egoity so fully that one can value others as one values oneself is the heart of the moral life, as understood by Christianity.[7]

Spiritual growth, then, involves one in the personal struggle, stimulated and supported by God, to overcome a deep-seated narcissistic orientation and to live in intimate, loving communion with God, other people and creation. This view of spirituality will be given a more specifically Christian context later in this chapter and throughout the rest of the book.[8] But initially I will illustrate the view in a more general and cross-cultural fashion, focusing especially on the significance of the enhancement and expression of compassionate love through spiritual transformation.

Transformative suffering and healing

Emotional and moral integration and growth are closely connected to this spiritual ideal of self-transformation. Resentment, hatred, and fear, for example, inhibit positive spiritual change. These are self-isolating modes of consciousness which restrict one's openness to the realities conducive to spiritual change. Compassion, love, and courage promote spiritual growth and are key aspects of the ideal. But suffering is intimately associated with all of these emotions and moral qualities. Suffering is a crucial feature of emotional and spiritual transformation. This is certainly not a view peculiar to western, Judeo-Christianized culture. Two different cross-cultural examples will help clarify the intimate relation between suffering and spiritual growth.

The first illustration is found in particular groups of Bushmen of the Kalahari desert. The Bushmen live an extremely peaceful and egalitarian life which stresses communal sharing in an economy which traditionally focuses on hunting and gathering. A most remarkable feature of their culture is the healing dance, a ritual which varies somewhat between groups. Here I am referring to the form it takes in the area of northeastern Namibia, amongst the groups of Bushmen called the 'Kung'.[9] Though lacking both strict formal structures and hierarchical caste, the healing ritual occurs regularly, depending on the need for healing as well as practical factors surrounding interest, available participants, and leisure time. It is characterized by clapping, singing, and dancing around a central fire throughout the evening and into the morning. For the Kung, the intention is to arouse in the healers of the group an altered state of consciousness called *kia*. This experience is marked most significantly by the experience of a powerful spiritual energy called *num*.

Appropriately stimulated, *num* is said to heat up and rise in a vapour form from the base of the spine into the lower part of the skull. At that point the healer experiences *kia*, an intensely emotional altered state, wherein the healer is said to travel to the spirit world, converse with spirits, or experience paranormal powers such as remote viewing, telepathy, or fire-walking. Throughout the process, the healer is supported by other members of the group and he or she moves to initiate *kia* in other healers. But most importantly, in *kia* the healer becomes intuitively aware of the illnesses of the other participants at the dance. She or he heals the sick by 'pulling' out the disease or struggling with the spirits that are causing the particular illness. The healer channels the activated *num*, which provides the healing energy. However, becoming a channel or medium for *num* is a very painful process which itself involves intense suffering. In each instance there occurs for the healer a death-like loss of self-consciousness, the fear of actual death (which apparently can happen), and an incredible searing pain in and around the stomach area.

One old Kung describes the emotional and physical process: 'As we enter kia, we fear death. We fear we may die and not come back!'

Another says: 'Your heart stops. You're dead. Your thoughts are nothing. You breathe with difficulty. You see things, num things; you see spirits killing people. You smell burning, rotten flesh. Then you heal, you pull sickness out. You heal, heal, heal. Then you live. Your eyeballs clear and you see people clearly.'[10] Richard Katz, who studied first hand the healing practices of the Kung people, describes the fear involved in *kia*, and the transformation involved in one's letting go into it:

> The heating up of one's num brings on certain painful and frightening changes, which are expressed in a physical, emotional, and cognitive way. Fear dominates during these changes. If the fear is met and overcome, if healers transcend the fear by dying, then they can accept these painful changes rather than being dominated by fear of them. They can transform these changes into vehicles that allow them to heal. ... The fear and pain of that boiling num, the terror of that passage, is faced and overcome as individuals die to themselves. From the death of the individual Kung personality, the rebirth of the Kung healer must come.[11]

In the Kung culture, spiritual transformation in *num* arises only through intense suffering. The healers must undergo an extremely painful immersion into a spiritual reality that transcends their normal self and environment. Not everyone undergoes the transformative ordeal to become a healer. But the inspiration for such painful undertakings is compassion for the sick. Their spiritual transformation is intimately interrelated to their compassionate empathy. It is only through such suffering that the transformed healer reduces the suffering of others. One old healer, Kau Dwa, says: 'The boiling num is painful and the work of healing is difficult. But that is what we have learned to do, and that is what we want to do. We drink num because we want to heal others of their sickness.'[12] Another comments: 'I go to the sick person and pull and pull him. And the next day he sees me and says, 'Toma Zho, I feel terrific.' And when I hear him say that, my heart is glad. I feel very happy to have helped him. We seek num so we can help people properly ... If I save his life, he says to me, 'You've saved my life,' and he's very happy and loves me.'[13]

Another hunting and gathering culture, the Negritos of the Zambales mountains in north central Luzon of the Phillipines, place a similar stress on the importance of suffering in emotional and spiritual healing. But in this context the focus is more on the patient than the healer, or rather on the patient's painful transformation in becoming a healer. Kilton Stewart, an American anthropologist, was struck in his field work by the astonishing parallels of the Negrito healing ceremonies to western psychoanalytic approaches. In group contexts, the persons who were suffering illness were taken through trance-state regressions, to re-encounter the source of their present ailments, under the guidance of the tribal shamans. Remarkably, they were advised by the shamans to transform the painful experience into a medium that might benefit themselves and other members of the tribe. Stewart describes vividly the general pattern of the ceremonies:

> The Negrito shaman directed the patient to bring back from the trance state a creative product in the form of music, rhythm, posture, and words. He was asked to stay in the painful event until some indwelling force, which the shamans called a spirit, supplied music for the words he heard from the spirit cave, put the words into some sort of meter like a poem, and attached this music and meter to a series of motor sets, muscular actions, and postures, which we call a dance.
> ... They were requesting that the area of the personality which had formerly expressed itself as conflict, rage, and migraine headache change itself into music, poetry, and dancing – on the spot, as it were. In the healing ceremony itself they were requesting that the subject transform the pain into that which was socially significant and beautiful. The astonishing thing was that the patient obligingly complied with their requests. Since he would reproduce the music, words, and dance on future occasions, whenever he asked the help of this newly acquired force or spirit, there was no danger that this new area of the personality, which he had conquered with the help of the ceremony, would slip back into the limbo of the subconscious and change itself again into pain after the ceremony was completed.[14]

So the original pain associated with present suffering is transformed through group therapy into something creative and positive, even nourishing to others. In the Negrito culture, it is only through such transformative suffering that one might become a shaman. But everyone is eligible, and group healing is a given and encouraged. Stewart writes how '[t]he very forces that made [the person] sick should become a will, an urge, a drive to heal others. Here healing was regarded not as a guild or priestcraft or secret knowledge, but as the social heritage of all who had suffered illness and received treatment.'[15]

Stewart notices parallels between Negrito practices and some contemporary therapeutic contexts in western culture. But perhaps closer parallels to Kung and Negrito beliefs and practices reside in contemporary Christian ministries in the area of demonic exorcisms and deliverances. Like the Kung and Negrito practices, these various ministries maintain beliefs in a spiritual world and spirits and their relation to the human spirit in both positive and negative ways. Since the 1970s, popular interest in exorcisms has increased dramatically in North America, including a rise in alleged demonic possessions, oppressions, and afflictions, as well as the establishment of various cross-denominational ministries in response to this current.[16]

Typically, these deliverance ministers set out initially to discover if a person suffering from a physical or emotional ailment is actually undergoing an invasion or attack by an evil spirit. In the general view, such an encounter can take a wide variety of forms: physical pains, distorted desires or obsessions, voices, commands, depression, anxiety, anger, etc. If a negative spirit is discerned, the minister will perform a deliverance ritual which is often creatively adapted from a traditional Roman Catholic rite of exorcism. The goal is to draw the demon clearly to consciousness and expel it from the person. In some cases, the deliverance involves considerable struggle, disorder, and drama, and when successful it appears clearly to provide relief and healing for the sufferer.

Michael Cuneo remains open to the possibility that spirits are actually behind the phenomena but he suggests that there are various cultural factors that can explain naturally the current popularity of deliverance ministries: news media and the film entertainment industry, which have stirred the imagination and sensationalized various cases; the penchant in North America for creating and embracing self-help groups, therapies, and religious syncretism; the contemporary desire for the quick fix to personal problems and issues, and for shifting responsibility away from oneself; and the placebo effect, in inducing positive effects simply by the hope and expectation of relief and healing. However, it is important to note that there are other sophisticated writers who are more open to the possibility that there exist actual spiritual entities which intrude upon humanity in negative ways, for example, M. Scott Peck and Donald Evans.[17] Morton Kelsey also presumes that evil spirits might play a significant part in such cases and he turns to Jungian psychology in understanding the phenomena within the framework of the archetypes of the collective unconscious. He suggests there exists 'destructive archetypal content' which is autonomous and manifestly evil, and leads to physical and mental illness.[18] Still, whether or not evil spirits are really behind some of the cases or none of them, the phenomenon clearly involves a large number of people who are undergoing much suffering.

In his extensive fieldwork on the subject, Cuneo encountered many humble, compassionate and intelligent deliverance ministers and exorcists. These people typically regard themselves, first and foremost, as healers who are called to minister compassionately to the whole person, quite apart from expelling demons. Cuneo observes the positive results:

> Thanks to the researches of cultural anthropology, we now know that traditional religio-magical methods of healing may sometimes be as effective in alleviating mental and emotional distress as modern, secular ones ... Over the past thirty years or so, tens of thousands of charismatics have availed themselves of the ritual [of deliverance], quite often in the hopes of gaining relief from such diverse problems as depression, anger, or sexual anxiety. And if their personal testimonies are to be believed, at least some of these people have come out considerably the better for it. In one way or another, arguably, deliverance has helped them combat despair or demoralization and given them incentive for improving their lives.[19]

In his research Cuneo does not stress the possible significance of love and compassion as actual healing energies in the dynamics of this kind of ministry. Regardless of the source of the problems these people experience, it seems likely to me that many people in their deliverance-healings are tapping into spiritual powers and energies, quite apart from placebo effects and subjective responses to the environment. As I mentioned in Chapter 1, an important claim I am making in this book is that one can receive positive healing energies from God and spirits and other human beings. In that regard, there are recent studies which indicate that intentional prayer can be a significant factor in responding effectively to the suffering of another.[20] It is important to keep in mind the major role compassion plays in the deliverance-healing movement, even if there is a great deal of distortion, self-deception and manipulation on the part of some or many of the participants.

Spiritual transformation, empathy and compassion

These religious-healing practices of the Kung and Negrito people and those of the exorcists and deliverance ministries in contemporary America might appear quite alien to many western readers. However, we can observe the dynamic of spiritual transformation unfolding for them, with special emphasis on the awakening and expression of compassion towards the suffering of others. In both the Kung and Negrito cultures, suffering is explicitly linked to physical and emotional integration. Traumatic suffering is overcome through a healing which itself is a very painful process. It involves the de-repression of painful feelings and openness to a power which transforms the suffering into something creative and positive. The healing makes the person feel and function better physically, emotionally, and mentally. It acts to stimulate self-integration. But the link of suffering to spiritual integration is also illustrated in how those who have transformed their illnesses are able and inclined to heal others. That is to say, suffering in a spiritual context is closely linked to the development and unfolding of empathy.

Empathy is the ability to reach out to another and feel her or his emotions – to relate to another person intimately through a sharing of their thoughts and feelings. Edith Stein stresses how empathy is like perception in that one's attention is focused outwardly on something other than the subject. However, empathy differs in that it involves an immediate feeling in a person of another person's experience, and not just a perception. In empathy one becomes 'the subject of the content [of the experience] in the original subject's place'.[21] Stein also contrasts empathetic feeling from what she calls 'contagion' or 'imitation', where we merely copy or mimic an experience that we observe, be it playfulness, joy, grief, sadness, etc. In imitation, it is only our own feelings involved in the experience. We are not really participating in the experience of another person, even if we are being carried away by our perception of it, into our own similar feelings. In contrast, in empathy, 'the actual feelings in us ... announce a foreign experience to us'. We feel another person's experience. So Stein defines empathy as 'the experience of foreign consciousness'.[22]

John Nelson, a spiritually oriented transpersonal therapist, argues that empathy is the most important feature of psychotherapy: 'As in other arrests of development, the goal [of long-term psychotherapy] is to restore the individual to a condition in which spiritual growth can resume. The key to this restoration of selfhood is empathy – a heartfelt way of observing, listening, and communicating that is the primary healing force in psychotherapy.'[23] But empathy can be closely linked to suffering. In Chapter 3 I will explore briefly how empathy in relation to suffering can be associated with distorted and even destructive feelings and actions. However, effective therapeutic practices require a compassionate awareness and openness to the painful feelings and experiences which are inhibiting the emotional and spiritual well-being of one's client. We see this clearly at play in the cases of the healers in the Kung and the Negrito cultures, and in some of the deliverance ministries currently in North America. The view seems to come down to the simple idea that the positive sharing in another's suffering can induce various forms of healing love.

Suffering can play a crucial role in moving people out of self-interested orientations and inspiring them to noble self-sacrifice in a heightened sensitivity to the needs of others. A vivid practical example both of this view and of this actual personal transformation is recounted in the Holocaust experiences of Viktor Frankl. Remarkably, given the extent of utterly destructive suffering undergone by so many victims of the Holocaust, Frankl writes of his own fortunate overcoming of some of his suffering in the midst of such horribly debilitating conditions: 'often it is just such an exceptionally difficult external situation which gives man the opportunity to grow spiritually beyond himself.'[24] He stresses the importance of struggling to find meaning within conditions of quite immense suffering – of transforming one's suffering through a self-transcendence that involves the surrender to a higher spiritual power. 'The more one forgets himself – by giving himself to a cause to serve or another person to love – the more human he is and the more he actualizes himself.'[25]

In *Letters to a Young Poet*, Rainer Maria Rilke observes the long and painful learning process required for the development of a healthy and mature sense of love: 'For one human being to love another human being: that is perhaps the most difficult task that has been entrusted to us, the ultimate task, the final test and proof, the work for which all other work is merely preparation. That is why young people, who are beginners in everything, are not yet *capable* of love: it is something they must learn. With their whole being, with all their forces, gathered around their solitary, anxious, upward-beating heart, they must learn to love.'[26]

Such youthful learning to love involves some extreme suffering. Along this line, Dorothee Soelle insists the 'capacity for love is strongest where it grows out of suffering'.[27] She writes, 'Suffering makes one more sensitive to the pain in the world. It can teach us to put forth a greater love for everything that exists.'[28] Similarly Pope John Paul II maintains that '[h]uman suffering evokes *compassion*'. 'Suffering seems to belong to man's transcendence: it is one of those points in which man is in a certain sense "destined" to go beyond himself, and he is called to this in a mysterious way.'[29]

The embodiment and expression of selfless love – a key aspect of spiritual growth – is intertwined with suffering. John Nelson depicts the process in terms of the conjunction of empathy and compassion:

> when empathy is coupled with compassion, it becomes the most potent force of healing. Together they epitomize the consciousness of the heart. Compassion is a readiness to respond to another's pain without resentment or aversion, coupled with the impulse to dissipate the suffering. Unlike pity, which separates self from others and prevents sharing pain, compassion brings inward the suffering of another as a reflection of one's own pain. It embraces all who know sorrow and invites them into our life. 'I truly understand that. I suffer with you. We share this as we would share our humanity' is the message of a compassionate heart. Yet this is not a passive or impotent suffering; it is one that mobilizes the healing love of the Spiritual Ground.[30]

Empathy is a feeling-along-with others. Compassion is a feeling-along-with the suffering of others through a framework of love. Genuine compassion involves an affectionate sharing of the suffering of another person, whereby the sufferer might feel the support and receive it in this interchange of love. The exchanged love literally soothes and consoles the sufferer, which stimulates healing. Oliver Davies notes along with Martha Nussbaum how the process of compassion involves on the part of the intentional agent a recognition of the suffering, a passionate feeling towards the sufferer and a volitional reaction to it.[31] Davies also notes along with Paul Riceour how typically compassion requires an action in response to the suffering, in order to distinguish it from pity.[32] I would add here how an effective action in response to suffering might simply be a silent heartfelt holding of compassionate space for the victim.

Traditionally, religions tend to place the source of this compassionate orientation in the heart. So one can speak meaningfully of 'heartfulness', 'tender-hearted', 'heartache', or 'broken-hearted', as various expressions of the experiences of love and its loss. As mentioned above, Rilke writes of a youthful learning to love by gathering the various forces of one's being around an 'upward-beating heart'. And St Paul, for example, proclaims to the Galatian community: 'As proof that you are children, God sent the spirit of his Son into our hearts, crying out, 'Abba, Father!' (*Galatians*: 4.6).

Some people insist this association of love with the heart is not merely metaphorical.[33] The intense feelings associated with compassionate love seem to generate originally and expand outward from the chest area of our bodies. Certain religious traditions of India have explored this phenomenon in some detail, referring to it as one of various levels of spiritual consciousness of the human being which they call 'chakras'.[34] Christian contemplatives might speak of this level of consciousness as the spiritual sense of the heart. It is thought to be the central medium of love. It is that through which an individual might connect empathetically in suffering with others. One Roman Catholic Hermeticist writes of the heart's ability to actually extend beyond the individual, thus expressing the spiritual feelings and their expansion associated with the subtle contact or connection one can feel with another through love. He observes that the spiritual centre of the heart is the only spiritual sense that 'is not attached to the organism', it 'can go out of it and live – by the exteriorisation of its 'petals,' which can be rayed outwards – with and in others'. In this way, he argues, the heart is 'simultaneously human and divine'.[35]

In this spiritual affinity with another person, the empathetic lover suffers with the sufferer, sharing the pain in a heartfelt connection that the sufferer can actually feel and appreciate, and upon which he can trustfully depend. So the therapist, or any compassionate consoler for that matter, must remain in some respects empathetically open to pain. More than this, though, a truly effective healer is in a sense a product of suffering. She herself must have suffered similarly in order to heal others effectively. She must have a background which enables her to wade continuously in and out of painful experiences, drawing on her empathetic feelings in relating to the patient in helpful, healing ways, able to reach out knowingly and fearlessly towards his pain. If she remains cool and detached, distanced from her client's experiences, or recoils in fear from the traumas or unconscious distortions of the client, healing will be very limited or not occur at all. Carl Jung comments on how the 'doctor is effective only when he himself is affected. "Only the wounded physician heals." But when the doctor wears his personality like a coat of armor, he has no effect.'[36]

This perspective on the importance of compassionate empathy in healing contexts extends far beyond formal western psychotherapeutic practices. It is something in which we have all participated to some degree or another in our sympathetic contact with suffering family members, friends and strangers. We have seen its importance in Christian deliverance ministries. It is at the heart of Christian spirituality. In commenting on the many healing miracles of Jesus cited by the New Testament writers, Morton Kelsey connects these activities with the priority Jesus gives to love in his teaching. This naturally leads to a stress in his ministry on compassion in responding to suffering: 'One of the most concrete ways of expressing that love is through concern about another's physical and emotional condition, and the removal of the torturing infirmities, physical hindrances, and mental and emotional illness.'[37] We have also seen this important connection of healing with empathetic love in the shamanic spirituality of the Kung and Negrito cultures. Michael Harner expresses this relation most clearly and extremely in reference to traditional shamanic practices:

> The shaman shows his patients that they are not emotionally and spiritually alone in their struggles against illness and death. The shaman shares his special powers and convinces his patients, on a deep level of consciousness, that another human is willing to offer up his own *self* to help them. The shaman's self-sacrifice calls forth a commensurate emotional commitment from his patients, a sense of obligation to struggle alongside the shaman to save one's self. Caring and curing go hand in hand.[38]

So we find the importance cross-culturally of compassionate suffering in the therapeutic healing that goes on in spiritual growth. I will explore the intricate dynamics between suffering, compassion and spiritual transformation a bit more deeply in Chapter 3. But in reading this passage about the shaman's self-sacrifice I was struck by the remarkable parallel of this therapeutic perspective to the fundamental teaching of Christian dogma. That is to say, Christianity is essentially shamanic in its understanding of God. The shaman is willing to offer up his own self to help the patient. Christ – the shaman God – sacrifices himself for the sake of humanity.

Indeed, in this view the suffering, death and Resurrection of Christ is seen as much more than a Christian appropriation from pagan religions of fertility rites that celebrate the cycle of death and life in nature. The focus in this sacrifice is not nature but Jesus' compassionate participation in human suffering. This provides a model which connects God to this facet of spiritual growth. Henri Nouwen writes how Jesus has made 'his own broken body the way to health, to liberation and new life. Thus like Jesus, he who proclaims liberation is called not only to care for his own wounds and the wounds of others, but also to make his wounds into a major source of his healing power.'[39] But how are we to understand this 'shamanic' power of Jesus in healing human suffering and in animating others with this divine compassion?

The Christian Hermeticist I quoted earlier remarks in this regard: 'The Christian world worships the Crucifix, i.e. the image expressing the paradox of almighty God reduced to a state of extreme powerlessness. ... One sees there the most perfect revelation of the God of love. ... The only Son of the eternal Father nailed to the cross *for our sake* – this is what is divinely impressed upon all open souls, including the robber crucified to the right. This impression is unforgettable and inexpressible.'[40]

The crucial element of this quote is that the Son is 'nailed to the cross *for our sake*'. In this view, the suffering and death of Jesus cannot be understood as merely substitutive, retributive punishment for an original sin which satisfies the cosmic justice of an omnipotent Judge. This would remove the relevance of Jesus completely from *present* human suffering. Rather, in the words of Michael Harner, Christ, like the shaman, 'is willing to offer up his own *self* to help' *all* of humanity. Dorothee Soelle observes: 'As pure history the story about Jesus has no overarching significance. It is only understood and appropriated when its continuation is understood. Jesus continues to die before our eyes; his death has not ended. He suffers wherever people are tormented.'[41] But how is this possible? What does this mean? What is its significance for present human suffering?

We will turn to these questions in Chapter 3. But before we can explore them we need first to understand compassionate, transformative suffering more deeply by contrasting it with stances which involve no empathy and those that I will call 'distorted' forms of empathy. All compassionate suffering involves the orientation of empathy with the subject of suffering. So apathy in relation to others, as a passionless or emotionless condition, is obviously a very different ideal, whether for humankind or God. However, there are other forms of passionate empathy aside from compassion. Sadism and masochism are forms of distorted empathy very different from compassionate empathy. Chapter 3 begins by exploring the contrast between apathy, distorted empathy (sadism and masochism) and compassion, as these function as various possible responses to the suffering of others. It then proposes some basic principles of a politics of compassion, before turning to the question surrounding the possible significance of the suffering, death and Resurrection of Christ for present human suffering.

'Dawn'
Toronto, 1997

3
Suffering and Christ

On Another's Sorrow

Can I see another's woe,
And not be in sorrow too?
Can I see another's grief,
And not seek for kind relief?

Can I see a falling tear,
And not feel my sorrow's share?
Can a father see his child
Weep, nor be with sorrow fill'd?

Can a mother sit and hear
An infant groan an infant fear?
No, no! never can it be!
Never, never can it be!

And can he who smiles on all
Hear the wren with sorrows small,
Hear the small bird's grief & care,
Hear the woes that infants bear,

And not sit beside the nest,
Pouring pity in their breast;
And not sit in the cradle near,
Weeping tear on infant's tear;

And not sit both night & day,
Wiping all our tears away?
O, no! never can it be!
Never, never can it be!

He doth give his joy to all;
He becomes an infant small;
He becomes a man of woe;
He doth feel the sorrow too.

Think not thou canst sigh a sigh
And thy maker is not by;
Think not thou canst weep a tear
And thy maker is not near.

O! he gives to us his joy
That our grief he may destroy;
Till our grief is fled and gone
He doth sit by us and moan.

William Blake[1]

If the Spirit of the one who raised Jesus from the dead dwells in you, the one who raised Christ from the dead will give life to your mortal bodies also, through his Spirit that dwells in you.

Romans 8: 11

Apathy, distorted empathy and compassion

Before responding directly to the questions about the significance of the suffering of Jesus for present human suffering, which I raised towards the end of Chapter 2, I will continue to develop ideas pertaining to compassion in relation to suffering and spiritual transformation, as these are modelled in the New Testament accounts of the life and teachings of Jesus. This analysis involves an exploration of the nature of apathy and various forms of distorted passion or emotion in relation to suffering. I will also explore briefly some basic principles of compassion, towards the development of a politics of compassion.

We saw in Chapter 2 how compassionate empathy is closely connected to suffering. However, typical responses to suffering can take one of three forms. One can respond to the suffering of another person either apathetically or in an empathy of a distorted nature or in an empathy of love, that is, compassion. Traditional Christian moral teaching stresses the last attitude as imperative to the Christian life. This is an existential bearing which is exemplified by the teachings and actions of Jesus. It is a core aspect of his ministry. Morton Kelsey writes: 'If Jesus had any one mission, it was to bring the power and healing of God's creative, loving Spirit to bear upon the moral, mental, and physical illnesses of the people around him.'² Marcus Borg observes how this basic Christian orientation is intertwined with the 'relationship to the Spirit of God … . It is an image of the Christian life that provides both direction and growth. For Jesus and Paul, life in the Spirit begins a deepening process of internal transformation whose central quality is compassion. Indeed, growth in compassion is the sign of growth in the life of the Spirit.'³ This view of a gradual spiritual transformation involving an ongoing embodiment of compassion was developed in Chapter 2, and I will return to the theme in a moment by relating human suffering directly to the suffering, death and Resurrection of Christ. However, I will begin with the contrasting attitudes of apathy and distorted empathy, stances that are alien to Christian compassion.

Most generally, apathy can be understood as an existential stance wherein people remain distant and remote from suffering and other intense passions or emotions, whether in themselves or in others. As a consequence of this suppression of their own feelings and of any impulse toward empathy with other people's feelings, they live limited and isolated lives. Dorothee Soelle observes how by acting apathetically people avoid sharing in the suffering experiences of others. But she notes a direct correlation between such avoidance of suffering and the absence of positive modes of emotional and spiritual consciousness:

> [Apathy] is understood as a social condition in which people are so dominated by the goal of avoiding suffering that it becomes a goal to avoid human relationships and contacts altogether. In so far as the experiences of suffering, the *pathai* (Greek for the things that happen to a person, misfortunes) of life are repressed, there is a corresponding disappearance of passion for life and of the strength and intensity of its joys. Without question this ideal bears the imprint of middle-class consciousness.⁴

Apathy is a powerful medium of physical, emotional, or moral isolationism, the distancing of self from affinity and relationship. As a common contemporary social condition which especially marks the western world, Soelle suggests that it typically includes a moral lassitude or weakness that people tend towards in order to avoid feeling their own emotional pain. Of course, there are more formal, philosophical 'Stoic' resignations which might involve high standards of virtue. But both kinds of apathy involve the repression of the passions and a cultivated indifference to feelings of pleasure and pain. So these kinds of apathy are directly opposed to Christian ideals of compassionate communion and a social orientation and activism that are grounded and driven by love.

Although the most obvious kind of apathy is simply observing with indifference the sufferings of others, there are other forms. One type of apathy involves the avoidance of such observation altogether and another includes the actual inflicting of suffering on others. In its most extreme forms, 'obedient' torturers work mechanically and bureaucratically within social frameworks, tormenting and killing with the sanction of the state or under orders of another established authority. Perhaps this was the case recently in the events surrounding the torture of prisoners in the Abu Ghraib prison by United States soldiers. 'Independent' torturers can also be apathetic, though very different in that they are wholly alienated from the rubrics of society. For them the absence of any moral–institutional references and responsibility are combined with an apathetic insensitivity towards others.

So apathy can take a passive or active form with respect to the suffering of others. The apathetic individual might simply observe without feeling the suffering of others, he might tend to avoid altogether such observations, or he might from this orientation of indifference actively contribute to the suffering of others. In the latter case, however, these kinds of apathetic suffering-producers need to be distinguished from people who inflict pain in a *passionate* way. As in the case of apathy, such passionate suffering-producers can be found both among socially legitimized civil servants and outlaw sociopaths. Indeed, there is a continuum from a cold and heartless apathy to the most intense sadistic or masochistic pleasure when causing or witnessing pain. Moreover, these orientations are not found only in cases of extremely immoral situations. Apathy and distorted passionate orientations towards the suffering of others are common stances that we have all experienced in others and in which we have participated at some point and to some degree or another.

Genuine empathy needs to be contrasted with apathy and sadism and masochism. As I defined it in Chapter 2, empathy is the experience of another's consciousness – it is a feeling-along-with-others. Apathy involves indifference to suffering, sadism involves pleasure from inflicting or observing another's suffering, and masochism involves pleasure in experiencing one's own suffering. However, empathy typically moves us to try to reduce suffering. It usually moves one to compassion. Although there are various grades and degrees of compassion, in its most complete form it is the projection of one's personality upon the consciousness of another person who is suffering, and experiencing, comprehending and actively responding to her or his suffering in a compassionate fashion – that is, within a consciousness of empathetic love.

However, a passionate response to suffering may be compassionate or it may be pathological. As Ivan so astutely observes in *The Brothers Karamazov*, 'In every man, of course, a beast lies hidden – the beast of rage, the beast of lustful heat at the screams of the tortured victim, the beast of lawlessness let off the chain.'[5] In such cases one empathizes passionately with the suffering of another out of motives of manipulative or destructive pleasure, rather than through a caring consciousness of love. Here the contrast to apathy is a feeling-along-with-others – empathy – but this empathy takes *pathological* forms. So the contrast to apathy can be either distorted empathy, which is sadism or masochism, or a genuine empathy, which can mean to feel sorrow or pity.[6] Yet, genuine empathy is compassion, which goes beyond simple pity in the sense that it is never contemptuous or scornful. Feelings of morbid pleasure are associated with distorted forms of empathy, while sympathetic pain is involved in the love of compassion. Sadism and masochism are passionate stances toward others where distorted pleasure is experienced in empathetic identification with their suffering-experiences. This is not at all restricted to independent and obedient torturers. It includes a satisfaction which in its less intense forms is as common, I would say, as apathetic stances towards suffering. However, often these feeling can go unnoticed and unacknowledged by the subject.

Determining in a particular instance an individual's place on the scale between apathy and distorted empathy and compassion is dependent upon assessing his or her ability to identify with either the suffering-producer or the victim and the nature of this identification. A person of apathetic consciousness will not relate at all to the victim or the producer of suffering. A person empathizing in a distorted way might identify ecstatically or even unconsciously with a suffering-producer's sadistic fervour ('In every man, of course, a beast lies hidden'), or perhaps morbidly with the victim's pain. But in all of these responses to suffering, he or she will thereby be unable to identify compassionately with the victim. She or he will remain isolated either in the numbness of indifference or in the morbid pleasures of distorted empathy. Moreover, one's feelings in these contexts can quickly shift and change. Sometimes a person moves from apathy either to sadism or masochism or to compassion in causing or witnessing the suffering of another. Sometimes the dynamic is reversed. Sometimes sadism or masochism becomes compassion. Sometimes compassion tragically lapses into sadism or masochism. However, the specific internal processes in these movements and struggles remain shrouded in the mysteries of human instinct, autonomy, moral consciousness, and faith.

As we saw in Chapter 2, some theories of spiritual transformation suppose a very difficult movement in the integration of a compassionate consciousness. At a practical level, one is urged to transform those passions associated with destructive orientations into a compassionate stance conducive to the spiritual fulfilment of self and others. Christianity espouses an imperative to wrestle with those inclinations and attitudes which tend towards a socio-moral isolationism – to overcome that which inhibits one from connecting with God and spiritual realities and other human beings in loving ways.

Toward a politics of compassion

So one is called to struggle to transform those negative attitudes that inhibit compassion in oneself in relation to the victims of destructive suffering. Modelled by Jesus, this paradigm of compassion in Christianity urges one not only to help people heal from their suffering, but also to work to counteract its occurrence, by changing harmful structures and systems of society. So far I have been focusing on the personal compassionate response towards individual victims, especially in contrast to responses of apathy and forms of distorted empathy. In the next section of this chapter I will explore also the significance of Jesus' own suffering and compassion in relation to present human suffering. However, now I will explore the question of a politics of compassion.

In his explorations of the theme of compassion in the New Testament writings, Marcus Borg observes how this paradigm of Christian compassion is intended socio-politically within the Church and not merely personally and individually. He suggests further that compassion ought to be put forth in society as 'a paradigm of public policy'. He writes, 'In the midst of our modern culture, it is important for those of us who would be faithful to Jesus to think and speak of a politics of compassion not only within the church but as a paradigm for shaping the political order. A politics of compassion as the paradigm for shaping our national life would produce a social system different in many ways from that generated by our recent history.'[7]

In Chapter 5 I will contrast the paradigm of compassion with a paradigm of justice in relation to afterlife possibilities. But it is important to note here how some contemporary Christian teachings on social justice begin to provide a theoretical framework for a politics of compassion, even if this has not become generated into common practice. Borg suggests that a politics of compassion would involve especially a stress on community in contrast to 'the dominant politics of individualism', including an emphasis on the ideas of 'covenant' and 'civic virtue'.[8] Some current Christian social teaching goes further than this in stressing the intrinsic value of the human person and its various implications. For example, especially in some of the twentieth-century writings of the Catholic bishops, the Church has taken formal positive stances on poverty and work.[9] The significance of these writings on social issues is often overlooked by critics who focus negatively on other Catholic teachings concerning sexuality, the role and status of women, the exclusivity of male ordained ministries, and the environment. However, Dorothee Soelle, for example, draws ecumenically and appreciatively upon Pope John Paul II's pastoral letter on work in support of her own feminist-liberation theology of work.[10]

Although technical details can be complicated, the essential points of these teachings are straightforward: the state, employer and employee are responsible for ensuring that a worker's employment meets sufficiently the material needs of the worker and his or her family. More than this, work must also contribute towards fulfilling the worker's needs 'for self-expression, responsibility, and creativity', as Dorothy Soelle describes the dynamic.[11] This includes one's potential ability to contribute productively to the common good of the community and society as a whole. These rights to creative and fulfilling work follow from one's inherent dignity and potential as a person, and from a basic spiritual interconnectedness and responsibility towards other people. They also extend significantly to basic human rights in the areas of education and health care. John Paul II argues how, through work, a person *'achieves fulfilment* as a human being and indeed, in a sense, becomes "more a human being"'.[12]

In this view, the various subjective factors of employment always have precedence over the objective realities associated with economic systems. Labour always has priority over capital: the working conditions of the worker are more significant than the wealth that is associated with the work, and it needs to contribute positively to the worker's creative fulfilment as a moral and spiritual person. This inversion of a fundamental principle of capitalism highlights the radical nature of these Christian social teachings on work. Employers typically just do not think that way and most workers themselves perceive their work not as meaningful in itself but solely as a means to draw a financial income which is to be applied in drawing meaning from other life-contexts. Perhaps this Christian teaching concerning the priority of labour over capital might function as a basic principle in the development of a politics of compassion. Indeed, if all employers and governments began seriously to create and structure working conditions around the personal and spiritual needs of the worker, the positive consequences would be immense. Combined with the institutionalization of what might be an even more basic principle – what Latin American liberation theologians call 'the preferential option for the poor' – the world would change in even more dramatic ways.[13] By placing firmly and formally at the forefront of political and economic planning and policy those who historically have been the powerless and voiceless in our societies, we would see a significant reduction in destructive suffering. However, neither of these basic Christian teachings find their way firmly into the institutional structures of contemporary capitalist societies. Indeed, as far as I can judge, this principle of the priority of the worker over the objective dimensions of work and its implications are rarely even the subject of homilies in Catholic liturgies, despite its adoption at official institutional levels of the Catholic Church.

Still, these basic principles of a politics of compassion are espoused within the Christian tradition, even if they are not institutionalized generally in public life. What we do not find within the Christian tradition is a healthy legacy concerning the status and role granted to women and in the Church's relationship with the environment. After centuries of sexual discrimination, there has recently been significant movement in some threads of theology towards ensuring gender-equality in the areas of education, employment, and ministerial vocations, even if patriarchal authorities of some Christian denominations need to awaken more fully from distortions which continue to limit their openness to the teaching and ministerial authority of women. Along with this is a heightened sensitivity towards the legitimacy and significance of feminine symbolism in scripture and theology, and to the spiritual needs of women, within a tradition that has been predominantly and sometimes very narrowly patriarchal in its focus.[14]

In regard to the environment, some theologians are beginning to acknowledge past failures to relate in compassionate ways to non-human life forms and the natural world. In this book I am focusing mainly on *human* suffering and I am assuming an anthropocentric orientation with which some readers might disagree. Nevertheless, even if human beings are thought to play a more significant role in this world, given their special dignity in contrast to other creatures as free, intelligent and morally responsible beings, this does not mean that other life forms do not have intrinsic worth and that other aspects of creation need not be treated with great care and respect. Since the 1960s there has been criticism raised against the Christian tradition in relation to our current environmental crisis. This crisis is manifesting itself today in extremely serious problems, such as species-extinction, deforestation and the rapid depletion and exhaustion of other natural resources, and various forms of pollution and its effects, including global warming. Major contributing factors are negative human attitudes that lead to excessive consumption and insensitive exploitation of non-human life-forms and natural resources. These attitudes have been combined in contemporary times with immense advances in technology, leading to massive destruction.

Some critics argue that these attitudes – arrogant superiority and callousness – follow from teachings in the book of *Genesis* and other biblical texts. Humanity, by being created in the 'image' and after the 'likeness' of God, acquires a special and superior status within creation (1:26). In this first creation myth, human creatures are told to 'Be fertile and multiply; fill the earth and subdue it. Have dominion over the fish of the sea, the birds of the air, and all the living things that move on the earth' (1:28). This theme, calling one to subdue and dominate other creatures and the natural environment, is echoed and reaffirmed in various ways in other Biblical scriptures.

In a short but influential article on this issue, Lynn White, Jr argues that this imperative has led us to regard ourselves as 'superior to nature, contemptuous of it, willing to use it for our slightest whim'.[15] In the Judeo-Christian west there has been a neglect of the interconnectedness and mutual interdependence of all aspects of creation. The misconception is that 'God planned all this explicitly for man's benefit and rule: *no item in the physical creation had any purpose save to serve man's purposes*'. White observes how 'Christianity, in absolute contrast to ancient paganism and Asia's religions ... not only established a dualism of man and nature but also insisted that *it is God's will that man exploit nature for his proper ends*'.[16]

Perhaps White in his critique neglects other major contributing factors in our current ecological crises, especially the role of secular economic principles and basic human selfishness, apart from the role of Judeo-Christian myths. Yet he seems correct in his assessment that 'we shall continue to have a worsening ecologic crisis until we reject the Christian axiom that nature has no reason for existence save to serve man'.[17] We can look to scripture also for inspiration in this possible shifting of attitudes. In a second creation myth in *Genesis*, the reader is told that humanity is created to *serve* creation: the first creature was 'settled' in the mythic 'garden of Eden, to cultivate and care for it' (2:15). This simple imperative 'to cultivate and care' seems quite a contrast from the command 'to subdue and dominate'. This theme of stewardship and co-creatorship in relationship to the natural world is reaffirmed and expanded in different threads within the Christian tradition, most notably perhaps in the spiritual teachings of St Francis of Assisi (twelfth century), even if it has not become a predominant motif.

More than this sense of responsibility towards nature, the spirituality of St Francis perhaps also suggests how the phenomena of the natural world might play an active role in the healing of the human spirit. For St Francis, nature is permeated by spiritual energy which manifests itself as aesthetic value and meaning. St Francis speaks of relating affectionately with 'Brother' sun and 'Sister' moon. Along this line, Edith Stein develops in her Christian phenomenology the idea of an 'objective spirit' permeating natural phenomena. This spirit in things can affect the subject of its experience in meaningful ways. For Stein, all created being has 'a *meaning*, and it is therefore in the broader sense of the term a spirit-filled structure and thus a structure through which the Creator Spirit speaks to the created spirit.'[18]

So, for example, a natural landscape might manifest a certain kind of beauty that a person can appreciate and find quite powerfully moving or one might be consoled spiritually by the affection one receives from one's dog or one's cat. Marian Maskulak describes and quotes Stein's view of objective spirit, how 'all of nature holds meaning from which something spiritual speaks ..."Their spiritual sense is that which is full of value in them, that which can enter into us, which can delight us, lift us up, inspire us".'[19] Thus, in response to human suffering, both St. Edith and St Francis would speak quite literally of God's compassion extending to us through aspects of the created world, how the natural world itself helps to heal human suffering.

Lynn White, Jr mentions the spirituality of St Francis as a possible alternative Christian view of our natural environment, and proposes him 'as a patron saint of ecologists'.[20] Currently some Christian theology is becoming more sensitive to the spiritual significance of non-human creatures and natural phenomena.[21] An effective politics of compassion needs to include principles inclusive of non-human life-forms and non-sentient matter, even if humanity continues to be regarded as more significant than other created phenomena. In this thinking, in contrast to other life forms, human beings acquire moral freedom, heightened intelligence, and special responsibilities as co-creators with God. As stewards of the earth, humans are called to be compassionate towards the suffering in all of creation, and not just towards human life-forms. Christian compassion calls one to work towards redefining attitudes, structures and institutions of human life in ways that will reduce the destructive suffering of all creation, and not just human suffering. These imperatives, at both the individual and political–institutional level, are modelled in the New Testament narratives by the life and teachings of Jesus.

However, Jesus is more than a teacher and inspiration of a politics of compassion. Jesus is more than an exemplar of compassionate action at the individual and social levels. His life and teachings provide also an active power in overcoming present human suffering. For some Christians, current suffering is not an experience disconnected from the Divine, but rather one within which the Divine has been *and continues* to be directly revealed. As Louis Dupré describes it: 'A divine response ... counteracts existing evil by constantly presenting us with new occasions for the accomplishment of good or the redemption of evil ... According to Christian doctrine, God himself had to provide both the means and the model of this conversion by suffering and dying under the power of evil.'[22]

The Passion and Resurrection of Christ

Louis Dupré's claim about the significance of Christ for human suffering brings us back to our questions concerning the significance of the suffering and death (Passion) and Resurrection of Christ, which we raised at the end of Chapter 2. Dupré's thoughts on these themes can begin to be drawn out by briefly comparing Christian and atheistic compassion. Unlike a person submerged in apathy or the distorted empathy of sadism or masochism, some Christians and some atheists are moved compassionately through their experience and witness of suffering. Indeed, their compassionate suffering positively influences their way of being and acting in the world.

I began to illustrate the psychic-spiritual dynamics behind such a movement in earlier chapters. Suffering can move one out of self-interested orientations and inspire noble self-sacrifice in a heightened sensitivity to the needs of others. One's orientation towards others and life in general can be coloured positively through one's own suffering, issuing in a deep caring compassion towards the sufferings of other people and creatures. This indicates the possibly transformative character of suffering in general, which can move positively Christians and atheists alike. Soelle observes: 'Suffering makes one more sensitive to the pain in the world. It can teach us to put forth a greater love for everything that exists. It is not decisive whether or not we ascribe to 'God' this change that suffering effects.'[23]

However, with respect to compassionate suffering, the difference between Christian and atheistic stances has to do with the way in which this character transformation is perceived and grounded. For a Christian, this transformation of consciousness can be centred in a worldview wherein the redemptive experience of suffering is the overriding point and purpose of life. Suffering itself is not the goal. Dorothee Soelle illustrates the masochism inherent in theological interpretations or imperatives that encourage a seeking of suffering for its own sake. This is a pathologically destructive pursuit of suffering because it brings one pleasure.[24] Actually, this distorted stance towards one's own suffering is much more pronounced in Christian practice than is usually recognized or acknowledged. Indeed, there is always the danger that one might identify (often unconsciously) with the pain of another (or the suffering of Christ) because the connection one feels empathetically brings him or her morbid pleasure. This masochistic form of pathological passion leads the empathetic person to wallow narcissistically in his or her suffering. But such an isolated stance is incompatible with compassion. In such a condition there can be no love generated nor any overcoming of another's suffering. Rather, Christians are called to strive to make good the evils of suffering, to transform the experienced pain positively, to move from empathy (a feeling-along-with-others), to a stance of compassion (a feeling-along-with-others through a framework of love).[25]

This transformative stance towards suffering is not controversial – it is prescribed by most theists and atheists alike. However, whereas the compassionate atheist simply chooses to regard suffering in this light of love and to live her life and transform her character in this way, the compassionate Christian quite literally grounds this perspective spiritually in her experience of God and creation, and she asserts this stance as imperative to life. The Christian God is one Who in suffering and death is reborn in divine Compassion and Love. Dermot Lane observes how for Christians the belief in a compassionate God 'carries with it not only divine solidarity with the suffering of others but also a divine energy that empowers us to do something about the suffering...'.[26] Life is the painful, ongoing movement in and towards living and actualizing this Love, to perceive and act in the world through the 'screen' of the redemptive event. In contrast to those extreme subjectivist views of spiritual experience that we developed in Chapter 1, it is one of continuously appropriating into the world not merely an *idea* but the very *presence* of a loving God. To repeat Soelle's provocative insight into this dynamic: 'As pure history the story about Jesus has no overarching significance. It is only understood and appropriated when its continuation is understood. Jesus continues to die before our eyes; his death has not ended. He suffers wherever people are tormented.'[27]

One way of understanding the Passion or sufferings of Christ without succumbing to apathy or the pathological passions of sadism and masochism is to suggest that in their suffering empathetic Christians can identify compassionately at various levels with Jesus, the way of God revealed to humankind. Jesus experiences a brutal, alienating rejection and pain, not simply an acknowledgement of suffering, but the actual heartaching experience of the reality. Suffering in this view, even for the God–man, is the basic stuff of life, painful experiences that are only redeemed in the power of divine Love. Charles B. Guignon notes the stress in Christian orthodox spirituality on kenoticism as it is modelled in the crucifixion event: '*Kenosis* refers to Christ's act of self-emptying – his submission to the most extreme humiliation and suffering in order to do the will of the Father. In Russian belief, this self-abasement and self-abnegation has set a model for all humanity. To live the kenotic way of life is to follow the example of Christ, accepting suffering in meekness and humility.'[28]

In suffering Christians can identify ideally with what is to them the founding principle and *purpose* of life. Suffering, then, is understood in relation to themes which look to a future goal or end for the final resolution of the problem of evil in relation to an omnipotent and all-living God. Suffering has a purpose. As I have already remarked in Chapter 2, Dorothy Soelle says humanity 'learns through suffering (*pathei manthanein*), experiences change, is directed towards wisdom'.[29] She observes further that the 'capacity for love is strongest where it grows out of suffering'.[30] Dostoevsky expresses this purpose of life through Father Zosima's mysterious visitor, who suggests: 'It's a spiritual, psychological process. To transform the world, to recreate it afresh, men must turn into another path psychologically. Until you have become really, in actual fact, a brother to everyone, brotherhood will not come to pass.'[31] For Dostoevsky, this 'spiritual, psychological process' is a movement 'through the period of isolation' within which humankind naturally finds itself, towards the 'promise' and 'image' of Christ. It culminates in a transformed consciousness and orientation in love.[32]

We are all guilty: we all tend to avoid kenotic suffering – we are all inclined towards narcissism, toward a moral and spiritual isolationism. Indeed, in each of us even a destructive 'beast lies hidden'. As I mentioned in Chapter 1, in response to the scepticism of Ivan's 'rebellion' in *The Brothers Karamazov*, Alyosha cries out: 'But there is a Being and He can forgive everything, all *and for all*, because He gave His innocent blood...'[33] The forgiveness here is embodied in the opportunity revealed to us through the crucifixion event. In Jesus, humanity is offered the occasion through suffering to ascend and participate in a God who is, in Soelle's words, 'the symbol for our unending capacity to love'.[34] However, more than just a symbol of our love, this participation in God is from some more spiritually oriented Christian perspectives not just a matter of ethical imitation or credal formulation or cognitive appropriation. It involves a spiritual connection at various levels of being and awareness, beginning fundamentally in the liturgical mysteries. One does not just identify with the stories or the ideas associated with Jesus, but rather one connects with the actual reality of his divine Presence. St Paul testifies how 'the one who raised Christ from the dead will give life to your mortal bodies also, through his Spirit that dwells in you' (*Romans* 8: 11).

The spiritual experience of Christ

David Power, a distinguished liturgical theologian, speaks of Christ 're-eventing' in the community through an ongoing remembrance in a sacramental practice that positively transforms human life. This is the expression of the living Christ through 'the creative reconstrual' of biblical narrative and popular religion, the 'ritual gathering and acting of the people', and 'the evangelical witness of the community'. Power writes: 'In the faith that remembers the sufferings of Jesus Christ, the just and innocent, Christian people but know that God is present in the midst of this suffering. They find the presence of God's Spirit in themselves and in their fellowship with the suffering through their communion in the sufferings of Christ and in the hope of that witness.'[35]

Henri Nouwen remarks how 'Jesus Christ himself is and remains the most radical manifestation of God's compassion.'[36] As disciples of Christ, Christians are called to become active vehicles or mediums of this compassionate presence of God. This involves various kinds of gathering in community to share in this call to service, to worship, and to inspire and strengthen each other in terms of this common mission and aspiration. 'It is in the Christian community that we can be open and receptive to the suffering of the world and offer it a compassionate response. For where people come together in Christ's name, he is present as the compassionate Lord.'[37]

For many Christians, this remembrance does not remain merely a matter of human beings in community imaging the presence of Jesus through common practices and beliefs. Ideally, Christ is felt in liturgy to literally reoccur in individuals and in community, through sacramental mysteries that reveal 'the presence of God's Spirit' to the participants of the paschal event (the sacrifice and communion). There is an active redemptive power in this compassion which provides a tremendous consolation at various psychic and spiritual planes of awareness, and a genuine regeneration of spirit through the Christian into daily life. Christ's presence enters into the Christian who re-enacts and re-experiences the Passion and Resurrection of Jesus.

So Henri Le Saux (Abhishiktānanda) writes of the spiritual power of the eucharistic liturgy in redeeming the suffering of the world: 'The rite recovers its meaning when it is no longer the commemoration of a past event, but in its *"anamnesis"* (memorial) takes up the whole cosmic order, the suffering on every side, the cry that springs from the heart of the unfortunate, the life that never stops, the nourishment ... which all beings are to each other.'[38] This prayer, then, can extend well beyond human suffering, to include 'the whole cosmic order', thereby drawing into its liturgical context the pain experienced by non-human life-forms and the damage and destruction we inevitably do to other phenomena of the natural world. Human suffering is redeemed in the Love of the Christ-experience which it helps to induce. In this view, suffering ideally culminates in compassionate love that has its source in the death and life of the Divine, in the *Passion* of God. *Passion* transforms into *compassion*. Zosima says: 'Brothers, love is a teacher; but one must know how to acquire it, for it is hard to acquire, it is dearly bought, it is won slowly by long labor. For we must love not only occasionally, for a moment, but forever.'[39] And we must extend this love beyond humanity, to include all of creation.

Ironically, love also leads to suffering. Meister Eckhart preaches 'suffering comes from love and affection'.[40] In contrast to apathy and the passions of distorted empathy, as we developed these attitudes earlier in this chapter, the empathy which is grounded in love requires an openness to suffering. The suffering is redeemed in the joy of love that such empathy further induces and advances in its tranformation into compassion. In love there is a joy of life that is gradually enhanced and expanded through a compassionate consciousness that is opened wider and wider to the world's heartache and its transformation. This is because the Divine is present in the world, accessible in the human transformation of suffering into good, and encountered in various degrees in this transformative movement, as one is gradually opened more and more to this divine Presence. So Louis Dupré argues: 'In giving birth to the finite, God himself inevitably assumes a certain passivity in regard to the autonomy of finite being, a passivity that may render Him vulnerable and that indeed, according to the Christian mystery of the Incarnation, has induced Him personally to share the very suffering of finite being.'[41] Pope John Paul II writes that 'Christ through His own salvific suffering is very much present in every human suffering, and can act from within that suffering by the powers of His Spirit of truth, His consoling Spirit.'[42]

Besides being evidenced in the thought of some contemporary liturgical theology, witness to this divine Presence is also an important theme in other spiritual theology. There is much testimony which in its appropriation of the spiritual Presence of Christ focuses on an awareness of the affective divine love and joy pervading human life and the world. Distinguishing 'contemplation' from other religious experiences, Thomas Merton speaks of an 'awareness and realization, even in some sense *experience*, of what each Christian obscurely believes: "It is now no longer I that live but Christ lives in me" '.[43] He says, contemplation 'is a deep resonance in the inmost center of our spirit in which our very life loses its separate voice and re-sounds with the majesty and the mercy of the Hidden and Living One. He answers Himself in us and this answer is divine life, divine creativity, making all things new'.[44] This contemplative state is the 'amazing intuitive grasp by which love gains certitude of God's creative and dynamic intervention in our daily life'.[45]

Merton in his writings explicitly distinguishes this experience of spiritual contemplation from mysticism. But Christian mystics tend to claim the possibility of an even greater spiritual opening and awakening to a personal Divine Who is immanent in one's self and creation.

They thus provide a spiritual focus to Christian theology which is very significant for theodicy in its stress on the divine Presence in the created world. Some Christian mystics relate the theme of suffering directly to spiritual experiences of divine immanence and consolation. With reference to Christ, the significance of this suffering is in the revelation to the sufferer that God suffers with her/him *now*. One can identify in one's own anguish with the suffering Jesus. There is a profound healing power that some spiritually minded Christians become aware of mystically – a consciousness arising from deep in one's heart of the very presence of Christ's own pained appreciation of our suffering, indeed of all human suffering.

This is one way, I think, in which we can begin to realize how our heart is 'simultaneously human and divine', as I mentioned in Chapter 2 in reference to the anonymous Christian Hermeticist. It is a consciousness of Jesus' deep sorrow for one's own heartache, which inexplicably consoles one in a radically healing way. It is not simply an awareness of Jesus' suffering, but rather a heartfelt appreciation of his *compassionate* suffering *for* us and *with* us. It is not merely the hope but rather the actual felt presence of God's suffering with one. This awareness quietly moves the sufferer into a profound and mysterious healing grief of self, and gives her the feeling and knowledge that she does not suffer alone, that God is willing to die for and with her – that Christ is present most intimately in her pain, that Christ is taking her gently through her pain.

I am reminded here of Julian of Norwich, who focuses so much on the suffering of Jesus in her revelations. Julian's entry into the mystery of Christ is primarily through her own compassion for Christ's suffering in his Passion, thus illustrating Eckhart's observation that I noted above, how 'suffering [might come] from love and affection'. One finds in Julian's compassion for the sufferings of Jesus a way out of narcissistic self-centredness, through active participation in the Passion of Christ. The images of the suffering Christ are a major theme of the sixteen 'showings' or visions she experiences and interprets in her writings. Her eighth revelation is a particularly vivid and detailed realization of the Passion-event. Her deep devotion to Christ accentuates the scene, and the pain nearly overwhelms her. Julian writes provocatively of consolatory experiences that are linked to these meditations on the Passion of Jesus. The compassion that draws one into the Passion of Christ is met ultimately and reciprocated by the compassion of God. Julian writes of how she 'saw a great oneing between Christ and ourselves', both in pain and in bliss.[46] Given his very nature as the God-man, Jesus in Julian's theology is the medium who heals the split in human nature between our substance, which is united to God, and our sensuality, which is naturally alienated from this core of our being.[47]

Provocatively mixing her metaphors of Passion and compassion, Julian images Jesus as a loving Mother, through whom human suffering can be overcome in spiritual union with God. With respect to Eucharistic liturgy, Jesus 'is compelled to feed us, for the precious love of his motherhood makes him a debtor to us. The mother may suckle her children with her own milk, but our precious Mother Jesus, he may feed us with himself. And he does this most courteously, with much tenderness, with the Blessed Sacrament that is our precious food of true life. And with all the sweet sacraments he sustains us with every mercy and grace.'[48] Continuing along this narrative of Passion and redemption, Julian insists that through the very wounds that he suffered Jesus might draw us into the divine Presence, leading us back through his suffering into God and Her healing and transfiguring power: 'The mother may lay the child tenderly to her breast, but our tender Mother Jesus, he may lead us homely into his blessed breast by his sweet open side and show within in part the Godhead and the joys of heaven, with spiritual certainty of endless bliss.'[49]

Similarly, St Ignatius of Loyola focuses very much in his spirituality on compassion for the Passion of Christ. In the Ignatian Spiritual Exercises, one whole week of the four-week-long retreat is devoted to this theme. In the third week, the retreatant or exercitant seeks to enter deeply into the paschal mystery by meditatively contemplating the details of the Passion narrative in terms of various sensory-imagery: tactile, odour, voiced, visual, and auditory. The idea is that through active contemplative imagination one might penetrate the suffering of Christ in a very embodied way.

Michael Ivens describes the transformative dynamic in line with our theme of compassion:

> In the case of the Third Week, this more intimate and participatory grace is commonly designated by the word *compassion* (literally, 'suffering with') … *compassion* consists in a certain spiritual empathy, such that the contemplation of the Passion is itself a passion for the one contemplating, a suffering which is ours but in and through which Christ makes us sharers in his own. It can exist only as a mode of intense love. It transforms one's perception of every meaning of the Passion and the quality of every response to it, and it is the key to the contemplative union-in-action by which

through the apostles Christ continues to labour and suffer in the mission of the Church in the world.[50]

In Ignatian spirituality, it is through compassion that one enters contemplatively into the Passion of Christ. But this identification with Christ's suffering finds its fulfilment in the meditative contemplation of the Resurrection narrative, which is the contemplative theme of the fourth and final week, and the culmination of the Exercises. It is propaedeutic to intimate, spiritual participation in the consolatory joy and strength of the risen Christ, which frames and colours and charges the apostolic service-mission of Ignatian spirituality.

Writing in a rather similar vein, Meister Eckhart argues that suffering culminates ideally in a transfigured perception and orientation in the world; that suffering might be continuously overcome in experiential communion with a God of infinite Love and Joy: 'This is why [Christ] says, "No one will take your joy from you" (*Jn.* 16: 22). Once I have really been transported in the divine being, God becomes mine and whatever he has. Hence he says, "I am God, your Lord" (*Ex.* 20: 2). Then I shall have true joy which neither sadness nor pain can take from me, because then I have been established in the divine being where suffering has no place. For we see that in God there is neither anger nor gloom, but rather love and joy.'[51] Or in another passage, he writes, 'If my suffering is in God and God sympathizes with me, how can suffering be painful to me then, if suffering loses its pain, and my pain is in God and my pain is God?'[52]

So the consolation in this identification with Jesus' compassionate suffering is profound. But, as I mentioned above, there is also the possibility of the spiritual awareness of the risen Christ, which I have heard some contemporary mystics refer to as the experience of the 'shamanic' Christ. Such an image of Christ as shaman echoes back to Chapter 2, where I quoted Michael Harner's description of how the 'shaman shares his special powers and convinces his patients, on a deep level of consciousness, that another human is willing to offer up his own *self* to help them'.[53] This awareness moves one out of, though never completely beyond, one's own pain and the consolation associated with the awareness of the suffering Christ, through to a much more actively compassionate stance towards others. Christ not only consoles, but he also empowers. Here Christ's energy permeates throughout one's body in a combination of various life-affirming and protecting powers. But these spiritual energies are linked and find their expression through the heart centre. It is a spiritually enlightened power which is contained and directed by compassionate love. In this context, one moves out of the isolated consolation of the suffering Christ, into a more active compassionate concern towards other human beings and the natural world, which, much like Thomas Merton's view of contemplation, is very assuring, joyful, and enlivening indeed.

Christ and spiritual transformation

But one's own suffering is never forgotten or transcended in this process of spiritual transformation. It is rather transmuted into an ongoing active concern for others. Through one's own suffering 'in Christ' one is spiritually moved, and able, to help and heal others in the way that it is modelled by and experienced spiritually in the compassionate Christ. Dorothee Soelle quotes Simone Weil to illustrate this crucial point: 'The Christian faith relates to suffering not merely as remover or consoler. It offers no "supernatural remedy for suffering" but strives for "a supernatural use for it." A person's wounds are not taken from him. Even the risen Christ still had his scars.'[54]

Indeed, as I argued in Chapter 2, the scars are indelibly linked to one's healing powers. Suffering is necessary for spiritual growth into compassionate love and it seems to be mysteriously present in the ideal. Grounded in love, empathy requires an openness to suffering. But the suffering is only redeemed in the joy of love that such empathy further induces and advances in its movement to compassion. In love there is a joy of life that is gradually enhanced and expanded through a compassionate consciousness that is opened wider and wider to the world's heartache and its transformation. In suffering with Christ, the Christian becomes spiritually linked to a redemptive power that ideally draws him/her into its cosmic healing work.

Evelyn Underhill makes this claim in reflecting on her own spiritual experiences of Eucharistic liturgy: 'Going to Communion this morning I saw so clearly all the suffering of the world and the self-giving of Christ to heal it – and [I saw also] that Communion and the life of [spiritual] union mean and involve taking one's own share in [the suffering of the world] – not *being* [merely] rescued and consoled, but being made into part of His rescuing and ever-sacrificed body. And in the sacramental life one accepts that obligation – joins the redeeming spirit-element of the Universe.'[55] Note how suffering and its redemption extends beyond the human context here, to include 'all the suffering of the world'.

Through spiritual identification with Christ, suffering is permeated by the love and joy of the divine Presence which is witnessed and experienced in creation. Grief becomes grounded in the awesome healing power of redemptive, divine Love. Re-eventing the Resurrection experience, the suffering Christian mystic is reborn out of the ego-death of kenotic crucifixion, into the loving light of new life. Underhill writes of 'being made into part of His rescuing and ever-sacrificed body'. Eckhart speaks often in his sermons of one's giving birth to the Son. He also preaches: 'If anyone had forsaken himself and denied himself altogether, nothing could be a cross or sorrow or suffering to him. It would all be happiness, joy and gladness, and he would come and truly follow God';[56] Soelle says: 'In mysticism, suffering is the object of burning love.' The 'mystics' question remains how people can come to accept grief as joy'. 'The more a person dies to self, "keeps himself in a state of suffering", the more receptive he is to the action of God';[57] or again, Eckhart in a most bewildering moment: 'In all truth, if a person were willing to suffer for God's sake and purely for his sake, and if all the suffering that all human beings had ever suffered and that the whole world had ever borne at one time were to fall on him or her, all this would not hurt the person, and it would not be hard for him or her because God would be carrying the burden.'[58]

Eckhart here is speaking of a radical condition of mystical union that goes well beyond the normal frame of reference of most spiritually minded people. Indeed, in illustrating the contemplative ideal I have been focusing here on some major figures of Christian spirituality – Merton, Eckhart, Julian, Ignatius, Dostoevsky and Underhill. However, as I mentioned initially, there are various levels and degrees of this spiritual experience of Christ, and it can occur in a wide variety of religious contexts. For most of us, the awareness of our mystical link with Christ's compassionate suffering and Resurrection is less consciously pronounced and normally remains relatively fragmented, only occasionally and briefly marking the intensity and clarity that is spoken of by the classical mystics I cite here. Nevertheless, tremendous spiritual consolation and strength are accessible to those who are opened to the compassion of Christ. The imperative is to struggle continuously to be open to a deeper participation in this paschal mystery.

Suffering, then, is granted in this Christian perspective a meaning and significance that is foreign to the atheist, even the most empathetic. This Christian view of suffering is coloured by the affective connection to a Divine Who is intimately linked to human suffering both historically and in the mystically-present. It is shaded by the purpose of love that Christians observe in life. The ideal of life is to perceive and act through the spiritual lens of active divine compassion and love, a medium which is grounded in the very nature of a living and passible Divine. It is seen as irrevocably linked with suffering.[59]

The human likeness of God is only achieved gradually, through the painful human experience and overcoming of suffering, a travail that requires a relatedness to others both for its experience and its transformation, through a kenotic self-opening to God and hence to others. It culminates in a spiritual union which stands in direct contrast to isolationist perspectives, which see oneself as over and apart from others and their suffering. In *The Brothers Karamazov*, Zosima insists that from the perspective of the Resurrection experience 'all is like an ocean, all is flowing and blending, a touch in one place sets up movement at the other end of the earth ... Love to throw yourself on the earth and kiss it. Kiss the earth and love it with an unceasing, consuming love. Love all men, love everything. Seek that rapture and ecstasy. Water the earth with the tears of your joy and love those tears.'[60]

Note the call here for compassion towards the whole natural environment, and not just suffering humanity. Charles Guignon suggests that this is the theological inclusiveness through which Dostoevsky, through Alyosha and Zosima, answers Ivan's criticisms of Christianity: there is a 'mystical vision of the cosmos as a sanctified totality' that stands over and against Ivan's critique and rejection of the world in all its evil.[61] This heightened spiritual perspective involves an interconnection and harmony in love, rather than the isolationism which follows from Ivan's 'rebellion'.

Ivan rejects this world. To accept life is to approve of its horrible atrocities. Zosima's perspective is an acceptance of this world, one that is grounded in a realization of underlying spiritual affinity. Notice how this entails a responsibility for everyone and a compassionate concern and action towards the redemption of the whole world's suffering. This gives the theme of suffering both an individual and cosmic purpose, implying a connection between one's own redemption and that of the rest of the world, including non-human elements. In so far as Christians perceive *or even hope* through the unifying medium of this sacred underlying connectedness, they are accomplices to *all* aspects of the world, including the horrible events described by Ivan in his 'rebellion'.

So, rather than rejecting the world, Zosima urges in response to Ivan's concerns a rejection of isolationism. Zosima advocates a transformation of self and the world in a regenerating love that is grounded in the very unifying vision it induces and charges: 'Love all God's creation, the whole and every grain of sand in it. Love every leaf, every ray of God's light. Love the animals, love the plants, love everything. If you love everything, you will perceive the divine mystery in things. Once you perceive it, you will begin to comprehend it better every day. And you will come at last to love the whole world with an all-embracing love.'[62] It is only in passionately and fully loving life within God's Light and Love that one will come to discern most clearly and fully its meaning.

Mystic love and the theodicy question

Soelle suggests that ideally in this Christian spiritual context the 'theodicy question is superseded ... by an unlimited love for reality'.[63] She seems to mean that in certain cases Christians become so connected with and imbued by the power of this love present in the world, that they cease to question the justice and wisdom of the Divine, even in the face of the most destructive suffering. In this regard Eckhart writes: 'saints may make so much progress that nothing can take them from God. Even though the heart of such a saint may be grieved that people are not in the state of grace, his or her will remains quite uniformly in God and says: "Lord, I belong to you and you to me!" Whatever may happen to such a person does not hinder his or her eternal happiness so long as the very peak of the spirit is not affected in the place where the spirit is united with God's most precious will.'[64]

Not all suffering is conducive to spiritual transformation. As I will describe them in Chapter 4, many painful experiences are and remain utterly destructive. Nevertheless, some mystic-saints remain so confidently charged in compassion and love that this destructive reality of evil does not count against their faith in divine providence. The problem of pointless or destructive evils – suffering so horrible and devastating that no transformative overcoming or even healing in this life is possible – is superseded in mystical experiences of unitive divine consolation. Eckhart suggests above that 'though the heart of such a saint may be so grieved that people are not in the state of grace', she or he will nevertheless remain firmly centred in the transforming love to which and within which she or he has been translated.

Features of this ideal are realized by these special characters, who exude from their very being a heightened spirituality wrought through the long labour of their own painful re-birthing in the context of evil.

These mystic-saints might seriously wonder about the destructive suffering at work in God's creation, but their elevated intimacy with the Divine secures a confidence well beyond those of us of normal consciousness, who lack such a constant and pronounced spiritual awareness and strength of the Divine. As authority figures, these mystic-saints actually confirm the purposes that ground this theme of suffering in Christian theodicy.[65] Indeed, they live the ideal, expressing in their own unique ways the active creativity, compassion and justice that issue from the very nature of the Divine in these unitive experiences. In Eckhart's imagery, they give birth to the Son in their own individual way.

Mystic-saints are not exclusive to the Christian tradition. Moreover, followers of many other spiritual paths echo profoundly this particular Christian mystical perspective in the way in which they compassionately respond to and overcome their own suffering and that of others. We have seen this illustrated in the Kung and Negrito cultures in Chapter 2, and it is clearly a major feature of various other religions. However, most other religious traditions do not ground this spiritual view of compassion ontologically in the creative source of existence.

As I mentioned in Chapter 1, Ivan Karamazov cannot accept this Christian God and purpose because so many people are consumed by their painful experiences. He even acknowledges the possibility that some individuals might indeed achieve the spiritual ideal. Ivan might well concede that a few special people do through their suffering overcome self-isolating orientations, therein transforming and integrating themselves in divine compassionate love for others and the divine Source, and experiencing the harmonious wisdom, joy, and power of this spiritual transformation. But at what cost? After all is said and done, the sad fact of the matter is that suffering contributes to the achievement of the spiritual ideal by only a very small minority of people. Indeed, there have been few mystic-saints strong enough to survive the arduous process associated with this view of spiritual development.

Ivan focuses in his 'rebellion' on the poor children, those innocent creatures who are tortured and murdered in a system where the purpose of life is supposed to be spiritual growth and transformation in freedom towards the creative harmony, joy and love of the divine life. Well, it is plainly obvious that, through no fault of their own, these children cannot effectively participate in this framework of spiritual development. Are we to understand them as lambs, sacrificed for those few mystic-saints who prove strong enough to survive the emotional and spiritual ordeals of this life? If we suggest that these poor children miraculously achieve their spiritual actuality or finality in a heavenly afterlife, then we bring into question the necessity of this spiritual scheme in the first place. Why must we struggle away on earth if our spiritual potential can be actualized miraculously in an afterlife? If God can achieve for us our spiritual potential apart from our own individual struggles against evil, then why doesn't She/He? Moreover, if we accept this spiritual framework, we become accomplices to the destructive suffering of these children. When we embrace such a spiritual scheme we too become intimately responsible for their horrors. If we accept God and God's purposes then we accept and affirm the atrocities that go along with them. Ironically, Christian love itself forces Ivan to reject the Christian spiritual framework. Out of compassion for the suffering children, he refuses to buy into a system that promotes such horrors, refuses to grant the mystical supersedence of the theodicy question. This problem of pointless, destructive suffering is the subject of Chapter 4.

'Tobiah's Fish'
Kensington, Maryland, 1998

4
Destructive Suffering

As he passed by he saw a man blind from birth. His disciples asked him, 'Rabbi, who sinned, this man or his parents, that he was born blind?' Jesus answered, 'Neither he nor his parents sinned; it is so that the works of God might be made visible through him.'

John 9: 1–4

Destructive suffering and spiritual experience

Not all suffering is transformative. Much suffering remains utterly destructive, insofar as we can discern its effects. Even if some people grow morally and spiritually in their responses to their own and other people's suffering, and some go on to become special exemplars of the transformative ideal, many people are simply overwhelmed by 'destructive suffering'. Many of them, especially children, are not *able* to grow through their suffering. There is much suffering that involves no possibility of spiritual transformation or self-fulfilment for the victim.

Extreme and overwhelming cases abound. A young girl is repeatedly raped and then murdered. Children slowly die from malnourishment while a helpless mother watches their lives gradually fade away. Despite the lesson of the holocaust, death camps still exist today. We are all familiar with such atrocities, even if the majority of us do not have to witness them firsthand. Yet we need not focus on such abominations. We have all experienced destructive evil of some sort or another, suffering which served no purpose, suffering from which we learned or gained nothing positive, suffering within which we could only persevere and hope for distraction or release, and from which we could only pray for healing and recovery.

This suffering is not 'redemptive', in the sense that it might be 'redeemed' in terms of some good that it might serve to achieve. Certainly it cannot be thought to contribute towards one's spiritual development. Indeed, it often hinders quite radically one's spiritual transformation. Although it might be so horrendous as to constitute reason to question the overall goodness of a person's life, 'destructive suffering' in this view is not necessarily 'horrendous evil', as Marilyn McCord Adams understands it.[1] It corresponds closely with Simone Weil's notion of 'affliction' ('*malheur*'), though I would include also certain less severe forms of suffering than Weil does in her idea of affliction.[2] Destructive suffering in this view is simply suffering which is and always remains non-redemptive for the person. It has no spiritually transformative impetus or context for the victim in question. Its experience is always 'destructive' in some sense or another for the victim (e.g. 'to pull or break down ... make useless, nullify'),[3] even if in most cases it does not completely devastate and paralyse the person. It is suffering from which one is unable to respond in positive ways. It contributes nothing to one's spiritual growth and can inhibit it. When I refer to 'redemptive suffering', on the other hand, I mean suffering which is spiritually transformative to the person. It contributes positively to a person's spiritual growth toward the religious ideal.

One of the hopes in Christian theodicy that I am defending here is that all people might be healed from their destructive suffering. It is the hope that one can be rescued from destructive suffering by God or other people, to experience healing and continue a spiritual journey for which such destructive suffering contributed nothing positive whatsoever or perhaps even inhibited. However, more than this recovery from destructive suffering, there is the additional hope in Christian theology for the redemption of all people. This involves a permanent shifting of one's narcissistic self-centredness to an intimate condition of graced and selfless love with God and others. Certain kinds of suffering are crucial to such a transformative dynamic.

So there is a distinction here between (i) destructive suffering, which diminishes and hinders the person in some way or another and for which there is no transformative impetus or response in the person (but where there will, we hope, be healing or recovery) and (ii) transformative suffering – that which contributes positively to personal growth – what we might call redemptive suffering. Given the complex web of human experience and growth it is sometimes very difficult to distinguish specific destructive from transformative or redemptive suffering, even within one's own life-experiences: some people are able to respond transformatively in certain cases of very extreme suffering; and in some instances it can take many years for people to discern or indeed to integrate for themselves and thereby realize the positive effects of certain radical suffering that initially appeared to be utterly destructive. So in some cases apparently destructive suffering turns out not to have been destructive – it is eventually transformed in positive ways. Moreover, Christians are called to attempt to transform all apparently destructive suffering.

However, clearly we all experience destructive suffering of some form or another. It is often not completely debilitating. It can range from the varying degrees of acute discomfort associated with head colds, toothache, and broken bones, to the more severe and chronic trauma of serious emotional and physical abuse and disease. Although sometimes these painful experiences can be transformative, they are often not. Indeed, the fact that destructive suffering in some form or another is such a common experience needs to be stressed in discussions regarding the relative merits or deficiencies of theodicy. When we speak of a 'theodicy question', we need to acknowledge honestly the problem of destructive suffering alongside the positively transformative nature of much suffering. How can one reconcile this former phenomenon with one's belief in, and experience of, an all-loving and most powerful Divine? Indeed, why should one even continue to struggle for such a theoretical reconciliation?

I have noted already how Dorothee Soelle speaks of the theodicy question being superseded by powerful spiritual experiences of love that the Christian receives in unitive connection with a compassionate God.[4] She is suggesting that in various kinds of spiritual experience, which I explored in Chapter 3, questions of the justice or wisdom or love of God in the face of evil become displaced by the affective content of the intimate encounter and awareness of God. The problem of the pervasive and destructive nature of so much of the world's suffering remains unanswered and, from Soelle's perspective, quite legitimately pushed aside as irrelevant to the immensely positive reality of spiritual experience.

The most immediate difficulty with such a stance is that it skirts the very issue which hinders many people from opening themselves up to spiritually healing or transformative experiences. How does one give oneself in love to a God who oversees so much utterly destructive suffering? How does one surrender in their affliction to a God of love who apparently fails to show and give Her or His love to the many victims of utterly destructive suffering? This is the main question Ivan

Karamazov raises for theodicy in his rebellion against God in *The Brothers Karamazov*. But there is also the question of the integrity of views that suggest that the spiritual experience of divine love is sufficient to quell one's religious doubts in the face of immense evil. I would argue that abandoning completely the search for effective themes of theodicy involves certain negative implications both for theology and pastoral practice.

The question of abandoning theodicy

Terence Tilley argues that attempts in theodicy to reconcile the harsh experiences of suffering with conceptions of a theistic Divine callously efface the evil that it is. These moves in theodicy, he writes, 'create a reality in which what is truly evil is not evil',[5] insofar as they tend toward rationalizing and thereby *justifying* the horror that the person has endured. They also tend to inhibit imperatives to overcome suffering. Why, for example, if suffering is justified as conducive to spiritual transformation, ought another person act to remove the evil sources of such suffering? So Tilley claims that all theodicies ought to be abandoned because they involve assertive declarations that are evil, though he does not seem to advocate the abandonment of theistic belief in general.

These kinds of criticisms of theodicy are found also in Grace Jantzen's feminist critique of traditional themes in the philosophy of religion. Unlike Tilley, she advocates the abandonment not just of traditional theodicy but of what she calls 'the realist assumptions of onto-theology' pertaining to God.[6] She argues that traditional philosophical views of God as omnipotent, omniscient, and all-benevolent constitute a masculinist 'symbolic structure created by and for powerful white western men'.[7] With respect to theodicy, this symbolic structure makes the problem of evil 'an intellectual problem to be solved' rather than a practical, moral issue to be overcome. It prioritizes 'the onto-theological above the ethical'.[8] Theodicy explores questions pertaining to the nature of God in relation to the human doing and experiencing of evil. As such, it is an intellectual diversion which supports and even encourages repression and exploitation by the powerful towards the weak and vulnerable: 'the focus of attention is diverted within this presentation away from what human beings are doing or might be doing to inflict or prevent evil, away from the earth and into the transcendent realm. It [theodicy] is a study in necrophilia.'[9]

Jantzen proposes 'natality' as an alternative to what she considers the necrophilic symbolic structures of traditional Christian theology. In many ways this idea of natality functions like the principles of a politics of compassion that I proposed in Chapter 3. Natality is an imaginative vision or horizon that includes ideals of human creativity and flourishing, given within a general human aspiration to embody the Divine. So Jantzen advocates a fundamental shift in basic life-structures. Drawing on the work of Jacques Lacan, she speaks of overcoming a traditional masculinist symbolic of death, where the underlying patterns of meaning and value inspire orientations that are geared towards the after-life, are anti-body and disproportionately intellectual and abstract, and are associated with a social–moral neglect or lethargy.

In her vision of natality, the focus of philosophical theology shifts from transcendent concerns to the temporal and practical, from the afterlife to the this-worldy, and from the individual to the communal. The theological problem of evil, then, shifts from the question of divine responsibility to human culpability, and theological attention orbits around practical questions of compassion that pertain to the distribution of evil: who suffers, who victimizes, and how do we solve the problem? Jantzen writes: 'From a feminist perspective, becoming divine is inseparable from solidarity with human suffering: a symbolic of the divine is a symbolic of outrage, imagination and desire, and compassionate action, not the detached and objective intellectual stance which traditional philosophers of religion assume and which they take also to be characteristic of God.'[10]

So Professor Jantzen's view of natality prescribes a fundamental orientation of active love for the world which is manifested as compassion in the practical response to suffering. Philosophical theology that deviates from this basic stance is to be abandoned. Still, she does not go so far as to deny the relevance of all theoretical contexts in understanding theologically the problem of evil. Jantzen recognizes theory as a crucial feature of any credible life-orientation. She insists, however, that such intellectual speculation take the back seat to the compassionate 'engagement of suffering', and should be developed only to serve and encourage that practical, pastoral purpose. She writes: 'The struggle against suffering and injustice and towards flourishing takes precedence, beyond comparison, to the resolution of intellectual problems; and although it is important that the struggle is an intelligent one, there is no excuse for theory ever becoming a distraction from the struggle for justice itself.'[11]

Kenneth Surin, upon whose writings Jantzen is somewhat dependent, also espouses an imperative to the practical engagement of suffering, arguing that traditional theodicy has in fact been a distraction from appropriate pastoral concern. He proposes a 'practical theodicy,' insisting that 'holiness and conversion are the only authentically Christian responses to "the problem of evil".'[12] He stresses the theological claims of the compassion of God and God's participation in human suffering. The 'practical' questions for theodicy are what God and humanity are doing 'to overcome evil and suffering', not the 'putative resolution of the apparent difficulties that comprise its theoretical aspect'.[13] Indeed, he insists that the very abstract treatment of evil is the problem: 'To regard theodicy as a purely theoretical and scholarly exercise is to provide – albeit unwittingly – a tacit sanction of the myriad evils that exist on this planet.' It is to mediate 'a social and political practice which averts its gaze from the cruelties that exist in the world'.[14] Although Surin maintains a place for a practical theodicy which engages with particular evils, one which is 'articulated from the standpoint of the victims themselves', he advocates, like Tilley and Jantzen, the abandonment of theoretical theodicy, given its immoral implications.[15]

These religious critics of theodicy insist that theoretical theodicies tend to demean the traumatic experiences of victims. Their main argument seems to be that in justifying God in the face of evil, one inevitably denies the evil nature of the experience of victims, by making them somehow necessary to existence or positively constructive, hence instrumentally good. Their writings appear to be quite influential in contemporary theology,[16] and I am sympathetic to the general concerns that are raised by them. It seems clear that historically some themes in Christian theodicy have tended to belittle callously the incredible suffering that people undergo, or they have tended towards depicting the Divine as sadistic or even encouraged masochistic attitudes on the part of practising Christians. The work of these religious critics accentuates such distortions in some Christian theology. For example, we find these effects with certain atonement and faith-testing theories, and with extreme views of retributive punishment.

These critics of theodicy have especially underscored for me the importance in effective theodicy of distinguishing between destructive and transformative suffering, so that one does not lose sight of the radically negative reality of certain kinds of suffering for the victim. I will explore these themes further in the following sections of this chapter. However, I think that these critics are overstating their case against theoretical theodicy. The issues they raise do not mean that *all* themes of theodicy are doomed to failure or that theodicy itself is evil in principle. The issues simply suggest that theologians ought to do better.

I mentioned how Professor Surin insists that 'holiness and conversion are the only authentically Christian responses to "the problem of evil"'. No doubt this claim is true. But how does one give oneself in love to a God who oversees so much utterly destructive suffering? How does one respond to the harsh criticisms raised for theistic religion by atheistic sceptics?[17] More importantly, how can one maintain the character of one's own spiritual experiences and aspirations – the integrity of one's own 'holiness and conversion' – in the face of the immense pain undergone by some victims of extremely destructive suffering? Indeed, it would appear ironically that it is in abandoning completely the hope and search for effective themes in theoretical theodicy that one would be truly demeaning the victim's experience of extremely destructive suffering because one would be ruling out that which would ground and support that hope for the recovery and redemption of the victim.

What is one doing when one abandons theoretical theodicy *in principle*? In terms of the themes in this chapter, one would be claiming that it is impossible to reconcile in intelligible ways God's goodness, love, and power with the evil reality of destructive suffering. It is to maintain that the ideas associated with a most powerful God of love cannot co-exist with the experience of destructive suffering. However, one wonders how in such a radical abandonment one can ground one's hope in the healing and ultimate redemption of the victims. Surely a Christian needs to hope that God's goodness, love, and power are sufficient to overcome the effects of destructive suffering for the victims? One hopes in the rescue and ultimate redemption of the victims of destructive suffering by a most powerful God of love and justice. This is to hope for an effective theoretical theodicy.

The hope in theoretical theodicy is that the love, wisdom, and justice of God can be reconciled with the evils of destructive suffering. Perhaps the most significant aspect of such reconciliation is the healing and redemptive overcoming for the victims of destructive suffering, through the power of this God. A Christian theist hopes for this healing and redemptive overcoming for the victims, and effective themes of theodicy will give intelligible voice to it. It is one thing to suggest that this or that theme of theodicy is ineffective in giving voice to this hope. However, if one abandons theodicy altogether, then what is to ground one's hope in the healing and redemptive overcoming of the victims, in the face of radically destructive suffering?

Now, one might respond here by insisting on the distinction between the hope in the spiritual healing and redemption of the victims of radical evil by God and the hope in the theoretical articulation of that dynamic in the form of a theodicy. Someone might argue that one can abandon the latter hope in theoretical theodicy without abandoning the former hope for the victims. However, one can then ask what constitutes the basis or ground of this former hope for the healing and redemption of the victim? To respond to that question is to move (even inadvertently) towards the articulation of one or another theme of theoretical theodicy. Also related to this former hope, if there is such a healing and overcoming of evil by a God of infinite power and love, why should we presume this redemptive dynamic would be unintelligible? And if we can begin to articulate this dynamic, then so too we are moving into a theme of theoretical theodicy.

With respect to responding to victims of destructive suffering, Michael Scott argues: 'If any religious language is appropriate in such cases, it is not a shoring up of the theodicist's argument, but a renewed expression of faith, and this is something that the practical theodicist may facilitate by standing alongside the victim, by actively helping the victim.'[18] At one level, Scott's point is certainly true. In those pastoral situations one is called to attend compassionately to the victim of destructive suffering, not to speculate about theodicy. However, he is mistaken to suggest that 'a renewed expression of faith' has nothing to do with theoretical theodicy. Indeed, that which would ground and support such 'a renewed expression of faith' would be an aspect of theoretical theodicy. It would justify one's religious hope for the healing and redemption of the victims of extremely destructive suffering. So, for the sake of the victims, one ought at least to hope for effective themes of theodicy, even if one cannot claim to have these to hand. Moreover, this is an issue that applies generally to all contemporary theology that tends to minimize the power of God. There is the danger in such cases that the compassionate religious hope for the healing and redemption of the victims of extremely destructive suffering remains groundless and unsupported.

In exploring Dorothee Soelle's view on this issue, Professor Surin insightfully points out how Alyosha Karamazov, Ivan's brother and witness to Ivan's rebellion against God, 'follows the *practical* path of discipleship, in this way signifying his readiness to live without the metaphysical consolation of having an "answer" to the "problem of evil". Where Ivan turns towards heaven in accusation, Alyosha pursues an earthly *imitatio Christi* that involves solidarity with those who suffer.'[19] Nevertheless, Alyosha in the story never abandons *the hope* for the theoretical resolution of the problem of evil, as Surin advocates. How could he, without making a mockery of his solidarity with the victim? Insofar as Alyosha hopes for the healing and ultimate redemption of the victims, he at least hopes for the overcoming of their horrors by a God of infinite love and justice. Presumably this practical reconciliation, if it is to occur, would be theoretically intelligible.

The effects of destructive suffering

There remains the question of Dorothee Soelle's claim of how the theodicy question is superseded by powerful experiences of love that a Christian might experience in unitive connection with a compassionate God. In defending God in the face of evil, Louis Dupré notes how the 'believing philosopher' need only show that, within a given '*theological* context, belief in a good God is *compatible* with the existence of evil'.[20] The theological context that I am stressing here is the spiritual experience of some people that they are through Christ united with God's compassionate suffering for all humankind. As I argued it in Chapter 3, I think that certain spiritual experiences have a profound significance for theodicy. However, it is one thing to suggest reasonably in response to religious critics that they should take into account the relevance of religious experiences in evaluating theological responses to the problem of pain and suffering. It is quite another to backslide blindly into these non-rational mysteries *only when* this theological perspective becomes rationally problematic. If one chooses to abandon theodicy in this way then one forfeits theological cogency, and loses the moral legitimacy and honesty this implies.

I have also noted already in Chapter 1 Louis Dupré's observation that 'on the cross philosophy suffers shipwreck, believers and unbelievers unanimously declare'.[21] Now, an open and generous sceptic might allow the believing philosopher to suggest that suffering in the Christian context is only fully grasped in terms of a non-rational experience of the death and Resurrection of a mysterious Divine-man. Perhaps even Ivan, for example, might have allowed such a possibility in his dialogue with Alyosha. But even the most open-minded sceptic will not grant that this understanding of suffering grounded in the Christian experience of Jesus is simply displaced by love in the face of incredibly destructive suffering. They will rightly insist that even if many evils become meaningfully purposive within the Christian experience of spiritual transformation, many destructive evils remain.

Indeed, the most spiritually transformed persons – the mystic-saints of our world – will themselves respond to the problem from a practical standpoint with a confidence born from their consciousness of the intimate divine Presence, perhaps like Zosima and Alyosha in *The Brothers Karamazov*. But if they are also believing philosophers, even they ought to recognize the issue and seek to explain plausibly the problems pertaining to destructive suffering. The utterly destructive power of evil counts strongly against ideas associated with a theistic God, and it forces even the mystic-saint to continue to search for a satisfactory explanation for pointless evil despite her or his amazing consolations. Moreover, it pushes the believing philosopher who has not the affective assurance of the mystic-saint to seriously and honestly question divine providence. Indeed, for the sake of the victims of radically destructive suffering, it is crucial to hope for a theological framework which begins to show how belief in a most loving and gracious God might be compatible with the evil of destructive suffering.

In regard to this struggle for an intelligible theodicy, there seem to me three relevant comments to be made in defence of an emphasis in theodicy on the transformative nature of suffering.[22] Although none of these comments will be either individually or together adequate in justifying the particular experience of destructive suffering for the victim, they do begin to show the possible theological context of such evils. That is to say, they contribute to the coherence of a religious worldview, where spiritual growth is thought to involve a long and difficult personal striving, stimulated and supported by God, to transform a self-isolating narcissistic orientation into intimate, loving communion with God, other people, and creation. These observations are not attempts to transform destructive suffering into positive experiences for the victims, but rather are meant to give this suffering an intelligible context within a theistic perspective, *especially* to encourage in the midst of destructive suffering an openness to the powerfully healing experiences of a compassionate God of infinite love and light.

It is crucial to distinguish between the effects of destructive evil on victims and the positive role these effects sometimes play for empathetic observers. First, it is important to note that witnessing the destructive suffering of others can induce the most profound emotional states and moral attitudes. I can recall, for example, the powerful effect that an illustrated book on the Holocaust had upon me, when in the sixth grade I stumbled upon it in my school library. Until that moment, I had no knowledge of those horrors. It was a shocking experience which opened me to feelings – positive, I would say in retrospect

– that I had not known, and that affected the development of my character in very significant and sometimes painful ways. It seems clear that empathy in the face of such destructive suffering can push one to the very edges of selflessness; and the incredible sorrow induced can move the observer of those who suffer destructive evils to levels of compassionate love well beyond that of the witness of lesser forms of suffering. We are reminded here of Dorothee Soelle's insight, how '[s]uffering makes one more sensitive to the pain in the world. It can teach us to put forth a greater love for everything that exists'.[23]

Secondly, even the sheer possibility of tragedy has a bearing upon the dynamics of spiritual transformation. Would the successful ascent of a major peak bring the same satisfaction and depth of experience to the mountaineer if it involved no risk of life or limb? Would not the absence of tragic possibilities radically transform who we are, what we might become, and how we would experience life? Human character would lack the depth and integrity and the immense joy that it can come to have in a world within which one must respond to destructive suffering. The awareness of the possible sudden loss of one's good-fortune, one's health, or one's beloved brings an appreciation and passion to life-experience which would not otherwise obtain for a person. Although a world free from destructive suffering would lack the intense sorrows associated with such tragedies, it would also lack the intense joys which occur when things go well. A world without pointless evil would be one without also the various corresponding goods that arise *in response* both to the possibility and the actuality of such incredible outrages.

The critic of theodicy claims that such observations are callous and even cruel in the way that they tend to diminish the destructive suffering of victims of incredible evil. Indeed, notice how my tone shifted in the last page, in proposing a rather abstract argument that tends to bracket for the moment the actual immense pain that people experience, suffering which is in some cases literally, utterly devastating. Yet these comments in this context do not suppose that all destructive suffering is deserved nor that it is mysteriously transformative for the victims in question. It rather accentuates the tragedy of the moral–spiritual narrative, the dangers and harshness of life, and the importance of the human struggle to participate in the work towards guarding against evil and healing the effects of such destructive suffering. It also begins to tell one why these atrocities might have to be in our world.

Moreover, there is a third observation to consider. A conception of a world free from destructive suffering involves severe limitations on human freedom. Because *all* suffering would be transformative in a world absent of pointless evil, human beings could never themselves cause destructive suffering. However, what would such a world be like? Clearly in some ways it would be much better than the one we know. Moreover, perhaps people might still be able to participate in a spiritually transformative process in such an imagined world. Yet such a dynamic would certainly differ radically from that which is imagined in this paper. For this participation and the ideal would not be one that involves human beings *dignified* through their own responsible struggles with destructive evil.

Michael Washburn suggests that the 'magnitude of responsibility is a function of the scope of freedom: the wider the scope of freedom, the greater the magnitude of responsibility'.[24] Christians typically long and hope for the eventual participation of all human beings in a divine life, within which beings of graced and perfected integrity will creatively and joyfully contribute their own unique gifts, strengths and love. The vision is not one of obedient puppets or geese, faithfully observing external rules and regulations for fear of harsh reprisal or in hope of hedonistic reward. The Christian call often stresses a great deal of human responsibility in a transformative process which culminates in a divine life of immense dignity and ultimate value.

This point will be further expanded in Chapter 5, in the development of the idea of hell as a condition of radical contraction from the spiritual ideal. The possibility that an individual might choose indefinitely to maintain a condition of self-isolated absorption secures his or her absolute freedom, responsibility and culpability. In short, it ensures their integrity as moral beings. We can make a similar point here in regard to the destructive evil that arises from the actions of autonomous beings: If the depth of spiritual transformation in one's religious conversion to the divine life *requires* the freedom of individuals to choose to do radical evil, we cannot plead for a substitute possible world wherein *all* suffering would be of a positive, transformative nature.

The point in this defence here is that extreme affliction plays a role in inducing, intensifying, and expanding the human capacity to love for those who must bear witness and respond to its reality in others. In those cases, such suffering is not destructive for the observer. Observing and responding compassionately to destructive suffering stimulates a depth of experience and character which would not obtain in a world where such suffering could not happen. Moreover, the possibility of destructive suffering is required in a religious picture that stresses the importance of a very wide-ranging freedom and human dignity in the spiritual transformation of humanity.

Destructive suffering and afterlife possibilities

So destructive suffering might have a positive impact upon some empathetic witnesses and can be understood generally within the theological context of a life oriented in grace and freedom, undergoing spiritual transformation towards an ideal condition of intimate love and joy. *However, such a theological account of it does not make it an acceptable reality for those who are victimized by it.* It is one possible response, or at least the beginning of a response, to a person who, upon observing the immense suffering of our world, laments in despair and scepticism, 'Why such horrors in our world, God?' But it is not likely to be a helpful answer to the anguished cry of the person deeply *immersed* in this affliction, 'Why me, God?' or 'Why my loved one?' Indeed, there is always the danger of losing sight of the victims in the clouds of qualifying theological abstractions. Religious critics of theodicy are right to accentuate this danger. In this view of suffering, however, these experiences cannot be justified in those terms for the victims, given their very nature as *'destructive'*.

This is a great tragedy of our world: destructive suffering is a condition of the fundamental freedom that is essential to our spiritual transformation and redemption, yet its personal experience does not contribute towards this religious ideal and can even radically inhibit it. Although God might be able to bring some good out of destructive suffering, as I suggested in the previous section, we can only presume, if it is truly destructive, that it remains without transformative impetus for the victims of it – that it remains a great evil.

In the most severe destructive suffering, the victim is either literally destroyed or reduced to a state beyond spiritual transformation in this life. Indeed, suffering can quite naturally lead to overwhelming despair, resentment, and distrust toward God, attitudes opposite those that are crucial to the transformative ideal. The question of destructive suffering is Ivan's problem in *The Brothers Karamazov*, and it does not simply go away, even in the mystic participation in the providential confidence and wondrous joy of an underlying spiritual connectedness and harmony. To ignore or deny the relevance of this issue is to begin to withdraw the compassionate empathy these victims deserve and to move towards an apathetic or distortedly empathetic stance towards them, which I described on Chapter 3. Moreover, we need not focus solely on the victims to illustrate the problems in emphasizing transformative suffering as a theme of theodicy. The independent and obedient torturers characterized in Chapter 3 carry the same weight as the victims in considering the problem, for they themselves are also defeated through the suffering of their victims. In their evil orientations and actions – in their apathy or distorted empathy – they distance or perhaps even remove themselves from the spiritual dynamic. In terms of the Christian ideal outlined in this book, the destructive suffering of the victims affects the suffering-producers just as much as their victims.

However, in his 'rebellion' Ivan bears witness to this issue as it pertains to the victims and it is on this count that he returns his entrance ticket to this world of such profound suffering. He will not accept the Christian worldview on the grounds of the unexpiated blood of the many innocent victims. For the sake of those few mystic-saints who have come to realize the saving power of divine love, billions have succumbed to the harsh trials of suffering, never appropriating the Christian ideal which *accounts in this theodicy* for the experience of suffering. To suggest that the victims are finally rewarded in an afterlife is to undermine the theme of transformative suffering proposed in this book, including the redemptive power of the Cross. For what is the point of human suffering if redemption is an afterlife reward given to those who are unable to transform the painful experiences in this life? *Why* the horrible trials in the first place, if redemption can be realized without them?

Clearly, Christian theology requires further creative speculation about afterlife possibilities in order to move this theme of transformative suffering beyond the problem of destructive evil. If in response to Ivan's 'rebellion' one is to draw consistently upon transformative suffering as an effective theme in theodicy, one must acknowledge the redemptive power of the Divine not simply in terms of afterlife rewards (or punishments). Rather, one must postulate either a realm (or realms) of purgatory and/or a return in another embodiment to this environment through a reincarnation or rebirth, wherein further spiritual healing, learning, and growth might occur.

The point here is that the stress on transformation in this view of suffering – that is, on the potential of a graced, spiritual development in and through the experience and overcoming of suffering in self and others – *requires* the postulation of an afterlife wherein this process might continue after death. This postulate is necessary in response to the terrible pointless sufferings which remove so many individuals from the transformative dynamics of this realm of existence before they have reached the spiritual ideal. Saintly exemplars are few and far among the general mass of humanity who apparently remain distant from the redemptive ideal at the time of their death. The theological point of life that is being defended in this book is redemption through spiritual transformation. If the victims of destructive suffering are not to be unfairly removed from this possibility, there must be contexts of healing which give them further opportunities for transforming purification. What is required is a life-condition suitable to healing and continued spiritual development, so the destructive horror does not unjustly remove the victim *finally* or *permanently* from the redemptive dynamic.

Even in those cases of our own experience of destructive suffering, the most important point is that we have at some future time the opportunity to overcome the debilitating effects of the experiences. This is not to say that even such evils will inevitably become transformative or that the pain associated with destructive suffering will magically vanish and therefore there really is no pointless suffering. Indeed, although the Christian is called to help transform even apparently destructive suffering in constructive and creative ways, it would appear that we simply cannot transform certain extreme suffering into something positive. In some cases we cannot make our experiences of suffering have a point after all, however much we might wish to do so or hope to repress the pain. Nevertheless, we can hope that we might be rescued from such destructive suffering through a powerful, healing love, so that we might be able to continue our spiritual journey, however long, difficult and painful this process might be. We can hope for the ultimate spiritual redemption of all humanity without denying the reality of destructive suffering.

Effective theodicy must suggest conditions wherein one is not totally incapacitated by the detrimental experiences and thereby prevented in a complete and final way from spiritual development *in other contexts* of life-experience. It is to insist upon the redemptive power of Christ, despite the reality of destructive suffering; that there be future conditions of healing and further transformative opportunities, analogous to these conditions that many of us experience in this life with respect to utterly destructive evils. So it is not that even such suffering will be 'transformed into good' but rather that such suffering might be 'healed for the good'. Indeed, when human beings do heal from extremely traumatic experiences in this life, no one suggests that their original suffering was not destructively evil unless it actually possessed some transformative thrust. But not all suffering has transformative significance.

We all have our scars – we all have our crosses to bear. Similarly, postulating a future life of healing and further transformative opportunities does not transform into good the experiences in this life of radically destructive evil.[25] Nor is such an afterlife postulation necessarily a distorted diversion away from present suffering and 'into the transcendent realm'. It need not be, as Professor Jantzen might suggest, a necrophilic move stimulated by distorted symbolic structures of meaning. Death is a reality of life. It is a great mystery we all have to face. The destructive experience of suffering is in some cases clearly well beyond present restorative powers. Postulating an afterlife condition of healing and further transformative opportunities suggests an appropriate restorative context, analogous to the conditions of recovery from radical afflictions that occur in this life. It seems, then, rather to lean towards symbolic structures of natality rather than those of necrophilia, in Jantzen's sense of the distinction, in its hope of rehabilitated life within conditions of creative flourishing. Such afterlife speculation provides an intelligible narrative within which there might be genuine religious hope for the spiritual redemption of the victims, however difficult and painful that process might be.[26]

This hope *follows* from the silent discourse of *genuine compassion*, that which Kenneth Surin refers to as that 'inarticulate speech of the heart, a speech which [opens] itself to the mystery of God, a divine mystery which makes present the mystery of healing'.[27] However, this compassionate hope finds its articulations grounded within this theme of theodicy, especially as we illustrated it in Chapter 3. To the anguished cry of the person deeply immersed in affliction, 'why me, God?' or 'why my loved one?', one might thus respond hopefully and confidently, 'Christ does not and will not abandon you in your pain. He and his angels will hold you and guide you in your transition, will embrace you intimately, bathing your wounds in his infinite love and light, healing you gently.' Such a response becomes even more powerful and assured within the spiritual experiences of love that a Christian might experience in unitive connections with the suffering and the risen Christ. For this healing love can be directed or channelled to the victims of destructive suffering, and one can come gradually to open one's heart to this compassionate and resurrected God, even in one's own radical affliction.

The stress in traditional Christian theodicy upon the theme of punishment has tended towards a shocking neglect of the innocent victims of destructive suffering. Saints Augustine and Thomas Aquinas, for example, speculate that all the evils of humanity are ultimately a consequence of sin and the punishment for sin.[28] In such a worldview, destructive suffering is construed as justified punishment, directly for personal sin or indirectly for original sin. Morton Kelsey illustrates how a similar view of sickness is expressed in the Anglican Office of 'The Visitation of the Sick' in the *Book of Common Prayer* (1549). In this document God is depicted as overseeing all sickness as punishment. Sickness functions as 'correction and chastisement' and is conducive to repentance. This formal service suggests that all sickness is intended to nourish faith-development. This means, as Kelsey observes, the 'Christian minister is left with no healing function'.[29] In light of ideas and teachings like this, it is no wonder images of purgatory in western Christianity tend to ignore or neglect possible healing contexts for those who innocently suffer destructive evils.[30] It is indeed remarkable how traditional accounts of purgatory in the Christian west fail completely to respond compassionately to the victims of destructive suffering. Perhaps this aspect of Christian theology *has* been a study in necrophilia, as Jantzen conceives the issues. In such a view of sin, all destructive suffering is transformed into good. It is perceived as justified punishment which secures in its compensatory function for sin the ultimate goodness of creation. Religious critics of theodicy are quite right to question the integrity and moral status of such themes of theodicy.

However, the postulation of further realms of existence suitable for healing and continued spiritual transformation (as well as for appropriate reformative punishment) does not succumb to the same criticism.[31] The crucial point here is made by Friedrich von Hügel, that unless we suppose a miraculous intervention on the part of the Divine with respect to human redemption, it seems obvious that conditions very much like those of this realm of existence will be required for most of us in an afterlife context.[32] And the former supposition, as I mentioned above, defeats the view of transformative suffering espoused in this theological view. Why must we struggle away on earth if our spiritual potential can be actualized miraculously in an afterlife? If the Divine can achieve for us our spiritual potential wholly apart from our own autonomous struggles against evil, then why doesn't God do this prior to our experience of such extremely destructive suffering? Moreover, if *we accept* such a spiritual framework we become *accomplices* to the unredeemed suffering of others. Out of love for humanity, in solidarity especially with children who suffer destructive evil, Ivan in his rebellion refuses to accept such a worldview.

One way out of Ivan's dilemma is to postulate some context where those who succumb tragically to their suffering in this life are afforded further opportunities in another lifetime for healing and spiritual development – that there will be an ongoing movement towards God. Ivan, then, cannot criticize the Christian God for neglecting or ignoring or regarding as a means rather than an end in themselves those who are annihilated in their suffering. For the innocent children are not forgotten or sacrificed by the Divine in this worldview, at least no more than the rest of humanity who are recovering from their destructive suffering in this life. They too will have further opportunities to overcome the evils inflicted upon them, to have the wounds of their suffering healed and, like most of us who are alive today, to continue to move gradually, hopefully, painfully forward towards union with God.

In this perspective, destructive suffering is regarded in the manner typical of the general moral response to such events: with horror and outrage. The child or adult who succumbs to the suffering associated with such atrocities ought not, without evidence or reason, be regarded as a responsible culprit. Indeed, in such cases the responsible causes are often found in the apathy or sadistic or masochistic tendencies of human beings, which I explored in Chapter 3. Or perhaps it is a consequence of the element of chance associated with natural evils which plays such a large role in this 'soul-making' environment. One might very well wonder if God could not do better in terms of this latter root of some destructive tragedies – the major and pervasive natural evils which confront human life. But one can understand moral evil in terms of the essential importance of human freedom in the actualization of the spiritual ideal without thereby claiming that the human experience of destructive suffering is a good thing and should be permitted to endure. Indeed, Ivan might argue that human freedom, and hence the ideal, is not worth the price we have to pay in terms of destructive evils. However, in these views of a continued afterlife existence, the terms of the transaction are radically transformed, for the victims are not finally defeated by the destructive tragedy. One hopes for an appropriate healing environment and further redemptive opportunities in the context of this future life-journey.

This possibility does not entail responses of apathy or distorted empathy towards the victims of destructive suffering, and it does not turn such evils into good. It acknowledges that much suffering, as destructive, is utterly alien to the spiritual ideal and ought to be resisted at all costs. Moreover, some people might choose not to make a responsive movement towards this spiritual ideal. So such afterlife speculation does not provide a final solution to the question of theodicy in the sense of suggesting that all evil will in fact be ultimately redeemed as good. It only suggests that God provides further life-contexts wherein healing from incredible life-traumas might occur and further spiritual development might transpire. Indeed, this seems the only genuinely compassionate response to those who undergo destructive suffering. It is through such speculative possibilities that redemptive opportunities might continue and divine Love be defended in the face of evil – further occasions wherein one might freely overcome the negative effects of destructive suffering, and continue the very arduous transformative movement towards this spiritual ideal.

But this positive spiritual vision has a negative contrast. As I just mentioned, this ideal of spiritual transformation is pictured over and against the possibility that some people might choose against the spiritual ideal. This possibility of hell is a major theme of the final chapter, where we will also return to the question of the afterlife possibilities of purgatory and rebirth.

'**Honouring the Four Directions**'
Kensington, Maryland, 1998

5
Afterlife Beliefs

> Love is patient, love is kind. It is not jealous, [love] is not pompous, it is not inflated, it is not rude, it does not seek its own interests, it is not quick-tempered, it does not brood over injury, it does not rejoice over wrongdoing but rejoices with the truth. It bears all things, believes all things, hopes all things, endures all things. Love never fails.
>
> 1 Corinthians 13: 4–8

> Be compassionate, just as your Father is compassionate.
>
> Luke 6: 36[1]

Suffering and afterlife beliefs

When one considers the problem of evil in relation to an all-loving and all-powerful God one must take seriously the significant role suffering plays in spiritual transformation, as well as the importance of other features of spirituality. In particular, as I developed in Chapter 3, the suffering, death, and Resurrection of Jesus illustrate for Christians both how God is open to human suffering and, more significantly, how people in their suffering might relate and connect to God in spiritually intimate ways that are healing and life-giving. These encounters of the spiritual presence of God constitute a 'redemptive' dynamic which brings deep consolation and healing to those suffering severe affliction. But these experiences also ground and model a hope for human life and the afterlife. They indicate the possibly transformative nature of some suffering, how it can stimulate spiritual growth towards a very beautiful and practical ideal of compassionate divine love in spiritual intimacy with God, other human beings, and all of creation.

I have focused, then, on the spiritual experience of Christ, the relevance of this intimacy for human suffering, and on the connection of suffering to spiritual transformation. As I argued in Chapter 2, some suffering, indeed much suffering, stimulates hidden potentials and strengths and is a key feature of personal character development. With respect to spiritual growth, certain suffering is especially important to self-integration, to the transcendence of a basic self-contracting orientation, and in the human transformation to a spiritual ideal of personal wholeness. It plays a crucial role in inducing, intensifying, and expanding the human capacity to love. This love might then be creatively manifested in a very wide variety of ways according to individual strengths, vocations and interests. One fundamental imperative in Christianity is the call to establish and cultivate a compassionate orientation towards the suffering of others, both at a personal level and also through the institutional development of a politics of compassion. Such a deportment of compassion is one of the more significant positive consequences of transformative suffering.

I argued in Chapter 3 that the contrast to compassion in relation to the suffering of others is either apathy or the passions of sadism and masochism. These distorted orientations severely pervert and even destroy the potential of the human spirit. They are modes of self-isolating narcissism. Indeed, the opposite of the transformative ideal is the analogue of hell: a self-contraction or self-absorption which distances oneself from the integrating and unifying energies of passionate love, both divine and human. So the ideal in this spiritual narrative stresses very much the role of freedom in human life, and includes the possibilities of either spiritual transformation and growth or self-absorption and decline, depending upon one's attitudes, actions, and openness to human and divine love and spiritual transformation.

The most serious issue facing this spiritual narrative is the problem of destructive suffering – that is, severe affliction that has no transformative potential whatsoever. In Chapter 4 I sought to illustrate a narrative of hope for those who suffer extreme affliction. This is not the hope that their suffering will somehow be justified before God and thereby rendered something other than the evil that it is, but hope simply that leads to an openness to spiritual healing and the resumption of their journey towards a divine Life of intimate love and joy. This requires, in part, that current theology move towards further speculation regarding afterlife possibilities. Essential to contemporary Christian theology that aspires to be relevant and compelling is the hope both for a future afterlife healing of the effects of destructive suffering and further transformative opportunities in the human movement towards the spiritual ideal. Purgatory and rebirth or reincarnation are possible mediums or environments of this continuing redemptive dynamic. I am suggesting that a belief in a compassionate and omnipotent God requires such postulations.

This chapter will explore in more detail the nature and significance of these afterlife visions. It will also examine the relevance of the possibility of hell, and in that context the relation between compassion and punishment. As discussed in Chapter 4, one way of responding to the problem of destructive suffering in traditional Christian theology was to explain it in terms of justified punishment. However, Dorothee Soelle argues that any religious response to another's suffering that depicts God as 'tester' or just-punisher is one where the believer cannot identify compassionately with the suffering victim because God does not. She would seem to suggest that if one views the suffering of another person as just punishment by God then one is inclined towards a stance of apathy or distorted empathy.

Perhaps Soelle's general concern can be understood in terms of the categories of the moral framework I developed at the beginning of Chapter 3. One is unable to identify compassionately with the sufferer because one consciously or unconsciously (i) assumes an apathetic stance of indifference, or (ii) takes pleasure in identifying sadistically with the victim's pain or the suffering-producer's satisfaction, or (iii) identifies with the victim in a masochistic way. Soelle passionately rejects themes of theodicy that tend to explain suffering in terms of punishment by God. Commenting on this theme in the book of *Job*, she notes how Job's companions are explicitly reprimanded by God for suggesting that Job's sufferings are deserved. She argues: 'Actually the doctrine about the punitive nature of suffering, after the unequivocality of this rejection [in *Job*], needs to be silenced forever. It is almost incomprehensible that it has survived and been renewed again and again through the centuries within the framework of the same culture which produced the poem about Job. Job's friends don't die out!'[2]

Soelle criticizes all religious responses to evil that resort to punishment in distancing God from evil. I would not go so far as to rule out the significance of punishment altogether in understanding human suffering, but I do think her arguments helpfully illustrate the serious problems for theological views that claim that all suffering is a consequence of sin or the punishment for sin. Her thought on this also helps in reflecting on the most extreme and severe theme of punishment in the Christian tradition, the doctrine of hell. Is it to be rejected on the grounds that it contradicts and rules out Christian imperatives of compassion towards the sufferer? What is the status of compassion in relation to the doctrine of hell? How, indeed, are we to begin to imagine the nature of hell?

Exploring these questions will help us to discern further the interrelated dynamics of suffering and the forms of distorted empathy, compassion, and spiritual transformation. This will in turn help us to frame more carefully the afterlife possibilities of purgatory and rebirth that I began to develop in Chapter 4, and to bring this book to a close.

Hell and the questions of justice and compassion

Within the Christian tradition the doctrine of hell has received a variety of formulations, critiques and apologies.[3] Underlying the diverse views on the subject are three common assumptions: it is an everlasting condition of existence which is to be construed as justified punishment involving extreme suffering. Enlightenment and contemporary critiques of the belief rest upon the indictment of it as excessive, alienating and non-reformative punishment. Yet, despite these criticisms, as well as the move on the part of some contemporary theologians towards a view or a hope of universal salvation, it is still maintained officially as a dogma of the Roman Catholic and various Protestant Churches, and held today by a majority (60 per cent) of US citizens.[4]

Early in *The Brothers Karamazov*, Fyodor Karamazov reflects with his typically bombastic sarcasm on the nature of hell after he learns that his youngest son, Alyosha, intends to enter the local monastery. I quote Dostoevsky's picture at length here because I think it is helpful in making clear the issues I have in mind. He asks Alyosha:

> So you want to be a monk? ... Well, it's a good opportunity. You'll pray for us sinners; we have sinned too much here. I've always been thinking who would pray for me, and whether there's anyone in the world to do it ... It's impossible, I think, for the devils to forget to drag me down to hell with their hooks when I die. Then I wonder – hooks? Where would they get them? What of? Iron hooks? Where do they forge them? Have they a foundry there of some sort? The monks in the monastery probably believe that there's a ceiling in hell, for instance. Now I'm ready to believe in hell, but without a ceiling. It makes it more refined, more enlightened, more Lutheran that is. And, after all, what does it matter whether it has a ceiling or

hasn't? But, do you know, there's a damnable question involved in it? If there's no ceiling there can be no hooks, and if there are no hooks it all breaks down, which is unlikely again, for then there would be none to drag me down to hell, and if they don't drag me down what justice is there in the world? *Il faudrait les inventer*, those hooks, on purpose for me alone, for, if you only knew, Alyosha, what a blackguard I am.[5]

It is important to keep in mind that in this passage Fyodor is not overstating his own shortcomings. He is a most remarkable devil's advocate here – if there is anyone in the novel deserving of hell, he certainly stands at the forefront. Moreover, he raises in his own facetious way issues crucial to the doctrine. For one thing, it is questionable as to how far one can go in the use of temporal, natural imagery to accurately reflect such an extreme and otherworldly condition. Fyodor speaks of the problem of imagining physical hooks and foundries in a non-temporal and spiritual plane of existence which presumably *must* exclude causal chains and material conditions in the application and maintenance of pain. But there is also the question of our ability even to imagine a state of *endless* torment, given the conditions of pain as we know them. Although St Augustine, for example, argues adamantly that 'it is possible for living creatures to remain alive in the fire, being burnt without being consumed, feeling pain without incurring death', even he eventually admits that such a state of affairs requires 'a miracle of the omnipotent Creator'.[6] Fyodor Karamazov simply brings into question the fantastic degree of imaginative speculation that goes into many traditional accounts and the adequacy of such literalist interpretations. This leads the reader to wonder about the nature and conditions of such afterlife suffering, if such a state actually exists.

However, most critics of the dogma take offence more with Augustine's eagerness to attribute such a condition of punishment to the miraculous power of an omnipotent creator than with the difficulties of imagining a landscape of endless torture or the appropriateness of traditional constructs. How, they ask, is the idea of hell compatible with an all-benevolent and loving creator?

John Hick, one of the leading contemporary spokespersons for the doctrine of universal salvation (*apocatastasis*), writes, 'The objections to the doctrine of eternal torment which once seemed so weak and now seem so strong are well known: for a conscious creature to undergo physical and mental torture through unending time (if this is indeed conceivable) is horrible and disturbing beyond words; and the thought of such torment being deliberately inflicted by divine decree is totally incompatible with the idea of God as infinite love ...'[7] The main issues facing the doctrine of hell seem to run as follows: it supposes an infinite penalty for human sins which are committed in a relatively limited time-frame; it neglects in its extremism the reality of the various gradations of human good and evil; it excludes completely the idea of reformative punishment in its conception; and it binds evil and suffering permanently into a cosmic framework which is supposed to be ultimately good.

In contrast to hell, Professor Hick develops and refines a view of universal salvation which has its roots in the thinking of early Church figures such as Origen, Clement of Alexandria, and Gregory of Nyssa.[8] Indeed, the idea of hell raises most serious issues for religious responses to the problem of evil in that it brings into question the compassion of God. Is the reality of hell compatible with an omnipotent God who is also all-loving? Is it consistent with the Christian image of an infinitely compassionate Being? Is it compatible with the Christian imperative to compassion that we have explored in previous chapters? For Hick and some other contemporary theologians, this is the way in which the problem of theodicy seems to be formulated: reconciling the reality and experience of certain kinds of suffering with the conception of an omnipotent and *all-loving* deity. In such a context, the theological perspective is driven primarily by compassion. The theologian applies her own moral and emotional sense of compassion in thinking analogously about the problem of evil in relation to God. To put the point simply, compassion for the damned, in conjunction with the idea of omnipotence, leads to the rejection of the doctrine of hell.

It is interesting to note how Augustine himself recognized this compassionate impulse at work in the speculative theodicy of his times, what he refers to as errors 'promoted by tenderness of heart and human compassion'. He says, 'I am aware that I now have to engage in a debate, devoid of rancour, with those *compassionate* Christians who refuse to believe that the punishment of hell will be everlasting ... they hold that they [the damned] are to be set free after fixed limits of time have been passed, the periods being longer or shorter in proportion to the magnitude of their offences. On this subject the *most compassionate* of all was Origen.'[9]

Augustine depicts compassion as a character weakness and defect of critics of eternal punishment, as a kind of mawkish sentimentality which, he observes, masks 'a delusive impunity for their own disreputable lives'.[10] For Augustine, compassion actually inhibits the appropriate intellectual discernment of the issues. Attitudes toward hell should not be driven by moral feelings of compassion but rather primarily by ideas of *justice*. Fyodor Karamazov, in our earlier quote, makes the same point when he stresses in his mocking irony the problem associated with his own denial of traditional formulations of hell. He asks, 'if they don't drag me down [to hell] what justice is there in the world? *Il faudrait les inventer*, those hooks, on purpose for me alone, for if you only knew, Alyosha, what a blackguard I am'.

Indeed, the term 'theodicy' comes from the Greek *theos* (God) and *dike* (justice), suggesting formally the emphasis on the question of justice with respect to the problem of evil, rather than the issue of divine love. That is, in defending God against the problem of evil, the defence focuses more on the nature and significance of divine justice than on divine love. For Augustine, the question of hell is answered through a synthesis of various themes of theodicy, but it is primarily an issue of justice. It is understood as punishment that follows naturally and consistently from the misuse of freewill, one that contributes positively to an aesthetic vision which is, on the whole and from a transcendent perspective, good.[11]

Hell, then, is understood from this wider perspective of divine wisdom or providence as ultimately a good thing though clearly for those who must undergo the eternal torment it is and remains a most terrible evil. It secures that the moral evils committed by the wicked receive their proper expiation or atonement through retributive punishment. Its absence would bring into question divine justice and its presence secures the perfection of the universe. This kind of argument seems to resonate well, at least in its basic structure, with human feelings surrounding the principles of fair play, responsibility, and reparation. Morally sensitive people hope that criminals will be brought to justice and are likewise frustrated when apparent criminals beat the system.

Indeed, traditionally the intent of punishment is to produce various positive effects that conform to our sense of justice: the self-acknowledgement, confession, and apology of the malefactor for his or her wrongdoing; a sincere request for forgiveness; redress for the loss or harm incurred; and the amendment of the character defect which led to the misdeed. The idea that certain extremely cruel and remorseless individuals be simply pardoned and forgiven for their crimes seems a morally outrageous proposition. Still, one can ask in the case of hell if infinite punishment reasonably corresponds to finite misdeeds. We are, after all, speaking of a state of *permanent* torture as punishment for a series of finite misdeeds. Surely it seems more reasonable to demand a limited time-frame to afterlife punishments?

Augustine was aware of this concern. But he noticed a tension involved in suggesting that afterlife punishment be finite while afterlife beatitude be eternal. He writes: 'The phrases "eternal punishment" and "eternal life" are parallel and it would be absurd to use them in one and the same sentence to mean: "Eternal life will be infinite, while eternal punishment will have an end." Hence, because the eternal life of the saints will be endless, the eternal punishment also, for those condemned to it, will assuredly have no end.'[12] Or, to put the matter another way, if the positive conditions of an eternal afterlife are to be determined by the moral behaviour and practices of a single life-time, surely the negative conditions of hell ought to be determined in the same way and time-frame and applied to an eternal context.

Heaven and hell

We can begin to make the major issues associated with the idea of hell clearer by juxtaposing it in this way with the positive conditions of eternal life. Hell only becomes intelligible in contrast to heaven and must, at least in certain respects, be seen as its opposite.[13] For Augustine and many medieval Christian theologians, heaven and hell are perceived as conditions of incomparable bliss or pain. This contrast depends in significant part on interrelated reward–punishment schemes that secure the overall justice of the Divine. One's actions in life are taken into consideration in a final judgment in death which determines one's condition in the afterlife. Hugh of St Victor takes such a framework to a sadistic extreme, perceiving hell as a contrast that actually enhances the pleasure of the heavenly condition for the elect. He writes: 'The unjust will surely burn to some extent so that all the just in the Lord may see the joys that they receive and in those may look upon the punishments which they have evaded, in order that they may realize the more that they are richer in divine grace unto eternity, the more openly they see that those evils are punished unto eternity which they have overcome by His help.'[14]

The sadistic tenor of this passage is remarkable. Notice how in Hugh's view compassion is displaced by an attitude of self-righteous and self-oriented *satisfaction* and even pleasure towards the eternally damned. Augustine's perspective is, perhaps, not quite as extreme. He insists on an awareness of the elect of 'the eternal misery of the damned',[15] but only as part of a more general awareness of evil as a contrast to the good and without suggesting that their suffering is specially designed to enhance the beatific vision. Still, he too suggests quite explicitly and adamantly that compassion is not an appropriate attitude towards the damned. He seems to tend more towards a stance of apathy.

It is interesting to note how theodicies that are driven primarily by concerns for divine justice tend to depict the religious ideal in terms of reward–punishment schemes that faithfully record and measure an individual's obedience or disobedience to moral and religious law. In this view, retributive punishment is very important as expiation of evils committed in an earthly lifetime even though such atonement can have no reformative significance for the suffering individual in question because the punishment is of a permanent nature. At best, such unending suffering serves only to satisfy or compensate (somehow) for the injuries of the victims of the perpetrator's sins, or to harmonize (somehow) the cosmic moral order that the sins disrupted, or to act as deterrent for others.

But Christian *agape* typically demands, in Donald Evans' words, 'concern, reverence, personal involvement and acknowledgment of value'[16] of the person. The active application of torture, its endless character and non-reformative nature, rule out such compassionate stances towards the damned. Yet, compassion towards the suffering of others is at the heart of much Christian spirituality, and it is crucial, I think, to effective theodicy. As Peter Phan puts it in reference to significant contemporary Roman Catholic theology: 'We not only may but *must* hope for the salvation of all. Such a hope is not an idle posture but constitutes a moral imperative to act in such a way that all will be saved.'[17]

This Christian imperative to compassion can be firmly grounded in conceptions of the afterlife ideal. Traditionally this goal was thought to involve the overcoming of one's fallen concupiscence. Originally simply 'desire' oriented by creation towards God, concupiscence became distorted through human perversion into a fundamental self-orientation or self-consciousness which separates and distances oneself from God and from others. This idea of original sin seems similar to contemporary psycho-spiritual views of 'narcissism'. Narcissism is 'a defiant self-separation from the divine Source', a fundamental attitude or condition of existence wherein one tends to view and act in the world independently from God.[18] The point of human life, then, is the very painful transformation of a basic self-contracting desire which inhibits both one's awareness of an underlying ontological intimacy with divine love, as well as one's human embodiment and expression of this love. In Chapter 2 I outlined this dynamic of spiritual transformation in relation to the experience of suffering.

Typically in the Christian tradition, and certainly in Roman Catholicism, this ideal is thought to be modelled for humanity by Christ and by spiritual exemplars who have appropriated to a high degree in this lifetime the life and teachings of Christ. Certain mystic-saints express in their lives and words the affective, spiritualized perspective involved in such a transformation of human desire or passion into the divine likeness.[19] They speak of a unitive awareness and, ideally, the compassionate consciousness associated with such realizations. Karl Morrison describes this transformative dynamic generally in specific reference to two famous medieval mystics: 'Love is "the transforming of the desire into the loved thing itself", wrote Richard Rolle (ca. 1300–ca. 1349). "Every lover", he added, "is assimilated to the beloved. [The soul], completely absorbed in its longing to love Christ, and Christ alone, transforms itself into its Beloved". Meister Eckhart wrote, "the eye in which I see God is the same eye in which God sees me. My eye and the eye of God is one eye, and one vision or seeing, and one knowing, and one loving".'[20]

The point that Professor Morrison is making here in reference to Rolle and Eckhart is that the goal of life is something which is actualized only in the overcoming of one's weaknesses and failings. It involves a personal surrender and integration into the Divine of one's basic, passionate self-orientation. He calls this transformative dynamic 'identity through empathetic participation',[21] thus paralleling the reflections on suffering and compassion that I have developed in earlier chapters. In a radical, foundational freedom, one surrenders one's personal self-isolating desire to God, and hence to others, and allows this relationship in intimate love to shape the spiritual transformation of one's will.

In such views, spiritual liberation then is not properly a 'reward' to be had in an afterlife paradise for obedient moral behaviour but rather an afterlife condition which is a natural extension of one's spiritual consciousness *in this life-time*. Moreover, it is one that culminates only in the communal and embodied context of the resurrected life. Spiritual liberation reflects the ideal of spiritual transformation which I outlined in earlier chapters. As Baron F. von Hügel puts it: 'Heaven is not a necessary environment for not cheating in the sale of peas or potatoes, for not smashing street lamps, for not telling calumnies against one's wife or brother. But only Heaven furnishes the adequate environment for the elevation and expansion of spirit.'[22] The ideal is only understood as the natural culmination of the transformative dynamic undergone in this life-time.

However, notice how in such a conception of the Christian ideal the attitudes of apathy or self-righteous satisfaction or pleasure towards the damned that are espoused by Augustine and Hugh of St Victor respectively are impossible. The only appropriate stance towards the sufferer is the divine, compassionate love within which one has identified and which one espouses. Moreover, if we further apply this view of spiritual transformation to conceptions of hell we paint a radically different picture from that of souls actively and forever punished by God for their earthly disobedience. The compassionate consciousness that is experienced and expressed is contrasted rather by a particular state of consciousness that constitutes the condition of hell, one of self-isolated and distorted apathy or passionate empathy.

The Christian spiritual ideal to which I am referring here maintains the goal of a transformative movement to a unitive consciousness grounded in compassionate love. This is a very painful transformation of a self-isolating orientation into a fundamental communion with a compassionate God and connection in love with others. Hell is the opposite of such an ideal. According to the moral framework I outlined at the beginning of Chapter 3, it would involve a consciousness like that of an individual immersed either in the conditions of apathy or distorted empathy in their most extreme forms, insofar as these stances involve a self-isolation completely wanting in love. This is in stark contrast to the loving empathy involved in a compassionate connection to God and others. Just as certain mystic-saints provide the human analogue to this spiritual afterlife ideal, so do those human beings who are extremely apathetic or passionately sadistic and masochistic provide the appropriate analogue for hell.

The picture, then, in this view of hell which is driven by this ideal of spiritual compassion, is simply one of being unable to identify with others and God lovingly. Father Zosima's account in *The Brothers Karamazov* illustrates vividly this perspective:

> Fathers and teachers, I ponder 'What is hell?' I maintain that it is the suffering of being unable to love.
> ... For such, hell is voluntary and ever consuming; they are tortured by their own choice. For they have cursed themselves, cursing God and life. They live upon their vindictive pride like a starving

man in the desert sucking blood out of his own body. But they are never satisfied, and they refuse forgiveness, they curse God Who calls them. They cannot behold the living God without hatred, and they cry out that the God of life should be annihilated, that God should destroy Himself and His own creation. And they will burn in the fire of their own wrath for ever and yearn for death and annihilation. But they will not attain to death.[23]

Notice how such an afterlife vision does not conceive of the Divine as actively involved in the punishment of the wicked. Indeed, hell is rather a human construct which derives from a self-affirmation in radical moral evil. The causes and nature of those fallen souls are the sense of their own loss of potential divinity, the prideful self-isolating contraction, their awareness but refusal of the wondrous possibilities of surrendering, in personal freedom, one's self-isolated will to divine love, and connecting with God and others in a loving way. So they remain unfulfilled in a condition of extreme self-oriented dissatisfaction. According to von Hügel, 'The lost spirits will persist, according to the degree of their permanent self-willed defection from their supernatural call, in the varyingly all but complete self-centeredness and subjectivity of their self-elected earthly life.'[24]

The state of affairs is a negation of human potential and a lack of participation in divine Being. It is rather an inner emptiness than an externally imposed positive affliction, a denial of one's spiritual potential and possibilities.[25] This idea of hell is found in the writings of St Irenaeus,[26] and it parallels the views of Plotinus and the Pseudo-Dionysius, who speak of radical evil as non-being, a nothingness, or absolute formlessness. It is the way in which I would interpret George MacDonald's comment, 'The one principle of hell is "I am my own."'[27]

Purgatory, rebirth and the hope in universal salvation

In these views of the afterlife, hell is envisioned in contrast to the ideal of spiritual integration and expansion within conditions of divine love, which is the dynamic of spiritual transformation that I outlined in Chapter 2. It is a contraction from one's appropriate end – a self-isolated condition wherein punishment is understood as the natural extension of the distorted consciousness of apathy or pathological empathy of human beings who continue to choose not to participate in divine love. So the afterlife conditions of hell are given some intelligibility, and God is not depicted in a mode of actively applying pain.

However, even if hell is a state imposed by human beings on themselves, there still remains a serious issue of justice or fairness: only a minority of human beings seem *able* to respond to their suffering with undistorted consciousness, participating in divine love. Human freedom in this matter is, by and large, very restricted. So whether or not hell is divine punishment or self-imposed, its fairness is questionable. Most human beings seem incapable of avoiding moving to some extent into their own hell on earth.

Indeed, I have spoken of a this-worldly analogue of hell as a prideful self-isolating contraction where the individual freely refuses to participate in the creative, dependent intimacy of divine and human love. However, it appears that many of us have this experience forced upon us from the outside, so to speak. For example, in reflecting on his work with the disabled people of L'Arche communities, Jean Vanier observes what he calls a condition of 'loneliness', a word which does not capture the severity of the suffering he describes. It is a state of radical isolation that seems to correspond closely to the analogue of hell that I have proposed here. I quote him at some length to illustrate the point:

> I once visited a psychiatric hospital that was a kind of warehouse of human misery. Hundreds of children with severe disabilities were lying, neglected, on their cots. There was a deadly silence. Not one of them was crying. When they realize that nobody cares, that nobody will answer them, children no longer cry. It takes too much energy. We cry out only when there is hope that someone may hear us.
>
> Such loneliness is born of the most complete and utter depression, from the bottom of the deepest pit in which the human soul can find itself. The loneliness that engenders depression manifests itself as chaos. There is confusion, and coming out of this confusion there can be a desire for self-destruction, for death. So, loneliness can become agony, a scream of pain. There is no light, no consolation, no touch of peace and of the joy life brings. Such loneliness reveals the true meaning of chaos.
>
> Life no longer flows in recognizable patterns. For the person engulfed in this form of loneliness there is only emptiness, anguish, and inner agitation; there are no yearnings, no desires to be fulfilled, no desire to live. Such a person feels completely cut off from everyone and everything. It is a life turned in upon itself. All order is gone and those in this chaos are unable to relate or to listen to others. Their life seems to have no meaning. They live in complete confusion, closed up in themselves.

Thus loneliness can become such uncontrolled anguish that one can easily slip into the chaos of madness.[28]

Vanier has dedicated his life towards helping the intellectually disabled heal from such extreme conditions of affliction. But the point here is that the children he describes have not voluntarily chosen to live in this hell within which they find themselves. Indeed, one of the elements of the most severe kinds of destructive suffering is the total absence of God – the inability to feel the healing nourishment of love or hope of any kind. Simone Weil's insight into this dynamic of affliction is profound:

> Affliction causes God to be absent for a time, more absent than a dead man, more absent than light in the utter darkness of a cell. A kind of horror submerges the whole soul. During this absence there is nothing to love. What is terrible is that if, in this darkness where there is nothing to love, the soul ceases to love, God's absence becomes final. The soul has to go on loving in the void, or at least to go on wanting to love, though it may be only with an infinitesimal part of itself. Then, one day, God will come to show himself to this soul and to reveal the beauty of the world to it, as in the case of Job. But if the soul stops loving it falls, even in this life, into something which is almost equivalent to hell.
> That is why those who plunge men into affliction before they are prepared to receive it are killers of souls.[29]

The children who Vanier writes about are those victims of affliction who have been plunged into hell well before their time. He writes vividly of the immense difficulties they experience in becoming open to the healing energies they might receive from others and from God. One wonders about their chances of being able even 'to go on wanting to love' in such misery, when many of them have not experienced it at all in their young deplorable lives.

Marilyn McCord Adams, writing in a more abstract vein on this issue, points out how our human freedom is impaired by interconnected factors which severely distort our ability to grow spiritually. These are associated with various limitations of human nature. They include: the ignorance and weaknesses with which humans are born into life; the difficulties of constructing non-distorted views of self and others; the maladapted coping factors often received from others, which we internalize and form into habits in our attempts to deal with immense personal and social problems; and the enormous difficulties we experience in repairing these most serious handicaps to our human freedom and in moving forward towards Christian spiritual ideals. Adams writes: 'such impaired adult human agency is no more competent to be entrusted with its (individual or collective) eternal destiny than two-year-old agency is to be allowed choices that could result in its death or serious physical impairment'.[30] One is reminded here of Dostoevsky's Grand Inquisitor, who, in light of human weaknesses and limitations, 'saw that it is no great moral blessedness to attain perfection and freedom, if at the same time one gains the conviction that millions of God's creatures have been created as a mockery, that they will never be capable of using their freedom, that these poor rebels can never turn into giants to complete the tower, that it was not for such geese that the great idealist dreamt his dream of harmony.'[31]

Both Dostoevsky and Adams are focusing on certain conditions pertaining to the problem of destructive suffering. In Chapter 2 I emphasized that much suffering is transformative, that it can be understood to contribute positively to spiritual development. However, as we saw in Chapter 4, some suffering is utterly destructive. There I explored how it is to be understood in relation to the dynamics of spiritual transformation. But as it applies to the problem of impaired freedom in relation to hell, the issue takes the form of a dilemma. One might, through compassion for the destructive suffering of human beings, deny hell and propose a universal salvation. However, this would seem to rule out the ultimate responsibility and dignity people possess in relation to their own eternal destiny, for their salvation is absolutely certain. Or one might, in stressing the importance of human freedom in determining people's eternal destiny, maintain the possibility of hell. However, this would seem to deny divine compassion, in the face of the apparent impossibility of the spiritual transformation of some people in this lifetime, given the severe conditions of impaired freedom.

Clearly, one way out of this dilemma is to postulate an intermediate realm or a series of lives following this lifetime. Those who hold this view of hell as a self-isolating contraction from one's spiritual potential *must* maintain the possibility of a kind of purgatory or rebirth in line with the sketches of these ideas that I proposed in Chapter 4. That is, they must envision continued life-conditions that are appropriate to spiritual healing and transformation or regression in order to respond effectively to the problems of affliction that are illustrated so vividly by Jean Vanier and Simone Weil. It is simply a matter of justice for those innocent victims of overwhelming, destructive suffering.[32] This matter of justice does not pertain to the question of whether certain retributive punishment is required or fair because punishment is not at issue here. These young victims do not deserve punishment but require healing and further redemptive possibilities. Justice has rather to do here with opportunities for healing and spiritual growth or regression within the freedom of a distinctive person in relation to the religious ideal.

This supposes future life-conditions much like that which we experience in this life. As von Hügel describes it in reference to the graced transformation of distorted habits, inclinations, and attachments: 'Purgatory is thus, so far at least, a sheer fact for the soul in its relation to God during this life. But it is not reasonable to assume a radical change or supersession of so fundamental a spiritual law at the death of the body, except under the constraint of some very definite and unanswerable reason.'[33] More than this though, the postulations of purgatory or rebirth are *necessary* to answer to the issue that Professor Adams raises. Given the severe conditions of impaired freedom, a single lifetime seems clearly not for the vast majority of humanity an adequate time-frame for spiritual fulfilment or damnation, nor consistent with ideas of divine compassion. In their haunting silence, Jean Vanier's afflicted children cry out for future realms of healing and transformative growth! Moreover, it is important here to emphasize how this issue of impaired freedom applies also for those people who uphold an ideal of spiritual transformation within the context of a doctrine of universal salvation. Even for those who reject the possibility of hell, the conditions of impaired freedom require the postulation of future contexts of healing and spiritual development within which the ideal of universal salvation might be realized.

In Chapter 4 I briefly mentioned the significance of such afterlife possibilities in responding to the problem of destructive suffering. This speculation regarding purgatory and rebirth must stress the significance of an afterlife condition appropriate for healing and continued spiritual integration and transformation. This is in contrast to postulations of afterlife conditions of appropriate punishment in the rehabilitation of a disordered soul or for misdeeds of past-life incarnations as it is generally understood in traditional conceptions of purgatory and rebirth. This is very important. For example, traditional Roman Catholic theology speaks of the importance of 'purification' through purgatory. Even in this traditional context, afterlife purgation is viewed as a realm of spiritual transformation. As Dorothy L. Sayers points out, the traditional Catholic conception of 'Purgatory is not a system of Divine book-keeping – so many years for so much sin – but a process of spiritual improvement which is completed precisely when it is complete'.[34] Nevertheless, the stress in this theology has typically been on the condition of purgatory as consisting solely of painful suffering as atonement which stimulates and finalizes spiritual redemption of a soul.

The dynamics of spiritual transformation put forth in this book involve the compassionate overcoming of suffering in self and others in the gradual movement towards the human embodiment of the Divine. It is not simply purgative transformation through painful punishment.[35] Moreover, in cases of destructive tragedy, like the children described by Jean Vanier, no punishment seems justified at all because the suffering appears to be pointless. Indeed, victims of destructive suffering do not deserve punishment but rather require compassionate healing. What is needed is an opportunity to deal with the effects of one's destructive suffering in a positive way, one which was not possible in one's previous life-condition. In this regard we find speculation in the theology of the Christian east concerning a purgatory which involves a continued process of learning and spiritual maturation; and in theology of the Christian west there is a call for further articulation of the process of spiritual transformation in contemporary conceptions of purgatory.[36] For example, Dermot Lane reflects on the transformative dynamics presumed in the process of purgatory:

> To decentre the inward-looking self demands that we recentre an outward-looking self focused on the mystery of God. This reshaping and recentring is a process that takes time in this life; it does not happen all at once – even though the conversion to God is decisive. Whatever is left within that process at the time of death, whatever remains to be done or undone, whatever perdures of self-centredness within the human personality, is the primary concern of church teaching on Purgatory. Purgatory, therefore, is about finalising a process, or better, completing the divine–human relationship already decisively initiated by God in this life through grace and only gradually accepted from a human point of view in this life.[37]

Purgatory, understood most generally as an afterlife condition suitable for 'completing the divine–human relationship', is a postulate suitable for responding to the problem of destructive suffering. In this context we can imagine conditions of healing and continued spiritual transformation, as distinct from regarding purgatory exclusively as a realm of retributive punishment. In reform theology, this kind of postulation also finds some support from Paul Tillich.[38]

A similar issue pertains to traditional views of rebirth in Hinduism and to what is more strictly speaking called a 'rebecoming' in Buddhism. In these 'retributive' views of rebirth, all suffering is thought of as justified retribution for past evils committed by the sufferer in either this or past lifetimes according to the law of *karma* (action and its effects).[39] In this perspective, there is no unjustified suffering. Like the theme of retributive punishment in some traditional Christian theodicy – that all the evils of humanity arise from sin and the punishment for sin – these claims of retributive rebirth seem preposterous. In such a scenario, birth defects, incapacitating accidents, crippling diseases, the Holocaust, and all other atrocities are viewed as morally justified happenings. Not only is such a moral perspective radically counter-intuitive, but it also seems to lead directly to conditions of apathy or distorted empathy towards the victims, those destructive stances I discussed in Chapter 3.[40] Indeed, hardline versions of retributive rebirth seem wholly incongruous with the themes of compassionate suffering and spiritual growth I have developed here. Retributive rebirth implies an attitude of moral *satisfaction*, in its juridical sense, towards suffering victims, not compassionate empathy. It is hard to see how one can feel deep compassion towards a child who is suffering painfully from an incurable disease or is slowly tortured to death when one at the same time holds that she must be getting the retribution she or he deserves for past misdeeds.

However, we need not in the view of rebirth understand the non-redemptive horrors inflicted upon children as justified punishment for some past-life indiscretions on their part. The focus rather can be on rebirth as a vehicle of spiritual soul-making. In the speculation of traditional Jewish mysticism and in some modern Hinduism and Christian theology we find postulations of rebirth which envision a continued life existence in a future embodiment in this world, within which one's spiritual journey continues.[41] Rebirth is here understood not solely or even primarily as a vehicle of justified punishment but rather as a purposive medium of spiritual growth. Through rebirth one maintains the opportunity to develop the many positive attributes associated with an embodied personality, in a gradual moral, emotional, and spiritual integration and self-transcendence in communion with God.

The transformative dynamics of this picture of rebirth thus resemble those of the version of purgatory that I outlined above. Sri Aurobindo

Ghose stresses a soul-making rebirth of this kind and Keith Ward, for example, similarly describes a 'soterial model' drawn from Vaishnava devotionalism in Hindu spirituality. In such views, human life is seen 'as an opportunity for learning love, for learning to attend to the Lord, or for falling under the sway of the desire-led qualities of goodness, passion, and ignorance'.[42] Moreover, in Mahayana Buddhism the ideal of the Bodhisattva highlights this compassionate sense of rebirth. In rebecoming, the Bodhisattva is not being punished whatsoever but willingly postponing final liberation out of compassion for the suffering (duḥkha) of others. The Bodhisattva is reborn for the sake of helping all of humanity to achieve the spiritual ideal.[43]

These various afterlife possibilities of rebirth and purgatory are not envisioned solely or primarily as vehicles of punishment, in contrast to certain traditional views of these afterlife conditions. Punishment might be drawn into them by supposing the possibility that some future suffering will be a consequence of previous improprieties. Nevertheless, afterlife punishment has to be conceived in light of the compassionate and all-powerful nature of God and the transformative ideal. Reformative punishment thus becomes the essential element of the conception of justice in this religious picture. Perhaps it is possible to draw retributive punishment into this context, where some suffering is understood to serve somehow to compensate or redress for a particular crime or immoral act. Although I am not sure how one would go about clarifying or defending the dynamics of such recompense, I would not rule the possibility out, given the powerful human feelings that are often associated with retribution in this regard. However, if such suffering does serve a retributive function, to make up or atone for a particular misdeed, I would insist that conditions of compassion require that it occur only within a context that offers the opportunity of a positive response on the part of the sufferer towards the spiritual ideal. Retributive punishment, if it occurs, must be accompanied by a reformative component or function. The guilty party might choose not to respond transformatively to such 'reformative retribution', but compassion demands that these opportunities be given. It seems to me that this subservience of retributive punishment to a reformative ideal is crucial in order to satisfy conditions of divine love.[44]

However, with respect to the particular view of hell clarified here, it is important to stress how one can acknowledge in such extended afterlife contexts of spiritual development (be it purgatory or rebirth or both) the sufferer's own ultimate choice and responsibility for his or her existential condition in self-constricting narcissism. Moreover, *he or she might choose to maintain such an orientation indefinitely*, eternally languishing in his/her own immersion in self-isolationism. That is the possibility of hell. It is important that this *possibility* be included in one's theological framework. Not only is it consistent with the afterlife ideal and the human experience of the radically destructive nature of some evil, but it also secures the freedom, responsibility, and culpability of the individual in question with respect to her or his spiritual destiny and to crucial aspects of divine justice. Nevertheless, despite this possibility, one is called to hope compassionately for the salvation of all of humanity.

The hope of theodicy

These afterlife possibilities of purgatory, rebirth, heaven and hell are, of course, highly speculative postulations that are outlined here only in a very general way along lines that are consistent with my earlier reflections on suffering, compassion and spiritual transformation. Like all afterlife speculation, they function as postulates that follow from religiously moral considerations and spiritual experience, and they lack the kind of evidence normally expected in support of empirical truth claims. Moreover, there are significant philosophical and theological issues pertaining to the possible conditions of personal identity continuity, the nature of the post-environmental contexts, and the possible compatibility of some of these ideas with central Christian beliefs. However, I think there is, at least, a significant traditional framework in Christianity to support the version of purgatory proposed here; and at least some versions of soul-making rebirth appear to be more compatible with many central Christian teachings than some theologians presume, in suggesting conditions for further redemptive opportunities.[45] Also, although doctrines of purgatory and rebirth are not publicly verifiable, there is some evidence that might be interpreted to support the possibilities.[46] However, most important, in relation to the themes of suffering, compassion and spiritual transformation developed in this book, these ideas are consistent with divine love. They respect the fundamental freedom and unqualified dignity of the person and the hope for effective healing from severe affliction. They help one to remain compassionately open to an individual's pain and genuinely hopeful concerning his or her possible movement out of self-destructive orientations, however doubtful this might seem in the long run.

Nevertheless, even in such a framework of afterlife possibilities one can still move easily to attitudes of apathy and distorted empathy. One can shift away from compassion to stances of apathy or even sadistic or masochistic pleasure towards the sufferer's plight, just as one necessarily does in views that stress conditions of justice in a hardline reward–punishment scheme, where the punishment is wholly lacking in reformative possibilities. Indeed, the historical popularity of strictly retributive punishment as a theme of theodicy reveals a deep human inclination to avoid compassionate suffering. For both apathy and distorted empathy eliminate compassion: in identifying with the righteousness of the punisher, one tends to avoid the moral imperative to identify compassionately with the victim and thereby conveniently evades the pain involved in such a sympathetic position. Adding to this evasion of suffering, Donald Evans suggests that there might be an element of morbid satisfaction in identifying with the 'just' punisher: 'Many of us, perhaps all of us secretly, can empathize with the sadistic pleasure of the sadist. Indeed if his cruelty can seem to have a moral justice to it, we can enjoy seeing the Bad Guy being punished severely; if we *have* to see him as the Bad Guy because considerations of justice demand it, our hidden proneness to sadism is easier to conceal.'[47]

In responses to evil which stress the theme of punishment there is a danger that a person might tend toward apathetic or distorted empathetic perspectives with respect to the suffering of the victims. To guard against this danger, it is helpful to keep in mind simple criteria proposed by Dorothee Soelle concerning the status of various religious responses to the problem of evil. First, she rejects all moves in theodicy that tend towards theological sadism – those accounts that explicitly or implicitly depict the Divine as a sadist. She writes: 'The God who produces suffering and causes affliction becomes the glorious theme of a theology that directs our attention to the God who demands the impossible and tortures people – although this theology can, of course, show no devotion to such a God. There is little doubt that the Reformation strengthened theology's sadistic accents.'[48] Secondly, she criticizes the Christian masochism that is often connected to theological sadism. These are theological interpretations or imperatives wherein unconditional submission to suffering becomes 'a source of pleasure'.[49]

Judeo-Christian theologians have always been concerned about the question of human suffering in relation to a most powerful spiritual Being who is thought to care deeply about creation. In response to the question, theologians have sometimes moved to sadistic and masochistic stances. However, the rejection of such distorted religious responses to the problem of evil does not rule out the possibility of other effective themes in theodicy. Two of these, I have suggested, are transformative suffering and divine participation in suffering. In these themes of theodicy, suffering is not witnessed as a final, retributive solution to the problem of evil, but rather it is understood in a way that is consistent with and fulfils the conception of a God of infinite love and power.

Such a divine-compassion approach to suffering differs from that of some Christians who deliberately or inadvertently take apathetic, sadistic, or masochistic stances towards suffering. Those stances pose serious difficulties for theodicy, as we have seen in relation to some traditional conceptions of hell. We should also note that apathy has been associated with an ideal of tranquillity in some Christian theologies. Dorothee Soelle connects this Christian quietism historically with Stoic influences, citing as example the consolatories of the Middle Ages. Soelle writes, 'the source of calmness is no longer God but indifference; the absence of emotions brings people to a world-conquering coldness, which moves along with a tone of resignation'.[50] These perspectives are incompatible with the compassionate orientation towards suffering prescribed in other Christian theologies. In contrast to such quietistic views, Christianity is grounded historically in the compassionate response to emotional and physical pain. Suffering is a brute fact of existence, and for most Christians its overcoming is an essential imperative. An effective Christian response to the problem of suffering is one which prescribes compassion towards the victims of suffering and does not legitimize apathy, sadism or masochism in God or humankind.

The response that I am proposing in this book suggests that we need not be alone in our suffering – that we might be intimately consoled even in our worst heartache. I hope it encourages especially an openness to the various forms of spiritual healing that are available to us from God and spirits, other people and nature. Teachings in Christianity, as well as from many other spiritual traditions, call one then to extend to others this compassionate healing Spirit we receive, and to work toward developing a politics of compassion that would establish the structural conditions for the creative flourishing of all human life. We are called also to relate respectfully and in nourishing ways to non-human life forms and the natural world, to act to heal creatively the suffering of all creation.

These reflections on suffering at least begin to ground theoretically and intelligently such a compassionate engagement of suffering. They express an ideal of spiritual healing and transformation which we can hold out hopefully to people who become overwhelmed and paralysed by their suffering, like my friend who inspired this book.

Notes

1 Context and Issues

1. This danger of denying the reality of the human experience of evil in one's attempt to reconcile the reality of suffering with God's power and goodness has led to what James Wetzel calls 'a growing theological backlash'. 'Can Theodicy Be Avoided? The Claim of Unredeemed Evil', *Religious Studies*, Vol. 25 (1989), 1.
   Theodicy is the attempt to defend God in the face of the reality of evil. Contemporary 'theoretical' or 'speculative' theodicies have come under attack by some theologians. Among other concerns, they argue that to suggest in a theoretical theodicy that suffering might be understood to serve some positive spiritual purpose, as I had begun to suggest to my friend, is to callously efface the evil that it is. In the words of Terence Tilley, such moves in theodicy 'create a reality in which what is truly evil is not evil'. *The Evils of Theodicy* (Washington, DC: Georgetown University Press, 1991), p. 235. Kenneth Surin claims that 'To regard theodicy as a purely theoretical and scholarly exercise is to provide – albeit unwittingly – a tacit sanction of the myriad evils that exist on this planet.' *Theology and the Problem of Evil* (Oxford: Blackwell, 1986), p. 50. So these theologians argue that the very practice of theodicy ought to be abandoned. I explore this issue in some detail in Chapter 4.
2. Fyodor Dostoevsky, *The Brothers Karamazov*, the Garnett translation, revised by Ralph E. Matlaw (New York: W. W. Norton, 1976), p. 226.
3. Ibid., pp. 226–7.
4. Ibid., p. 227.
5. See, for example, Kenneth Surin, *Theology and the Problem of Evil*, pp. 96–105.
6. Louis Dupré, 'Evil – A Religious Mystery: A Plea for a More Inclusive Model of Theodicy', *Faith and Philosophy*, Vol. 7 (1990), 278.
7. Such views regarding the subjective nature of religious experience are often associated with what are called 'constructivist' or 'contextualist' understandings of mystical experience, though not all contextualist views entail this extreme kind of subjectivizing of religious experience. The contexualist perspective stresses the over-determining role of human categories of interpretation in all mystical experience. Steven Katz is perhaps the most influential proponent of an extreme contextualist perspective. Two significant anthologies pertaining to questions of interpretation and experience in mysticism are his *Mysticism and Philosophical Analysis* (London: Sheldon Press, 1978) and *Mysticism and Religious Traditions* (Oxford: Oxford University Press, 1983).
8. For more on the epistemology of this view of religious experience, which I call 'experiential-constructivism', see Michael Stoeber, *Theo-Monistic Mysticism: A Hindu Christian Comparison* (London: Macmillan Press, 1994),

esp. Chs 1 and 2. In that book I suggest that categories of experience (related to concepts, dispositions, tendencies, etc.) do indeed frame and even enter into the nature of most mystical experiences. But I also maintain that there is a content or effect of the experienced reality upon the experience, one which might impact on the mystic's categories of experience in significant ways.

In support of my claims concerning the realistic interpretation of religious language about God and various spiritual realities, see, for example, Phillip H. Wiebe, *God and Other Spirits: Intimations of Transcendence in Christian Experience* (New York: Oxford University Press, 2004); Caroline Franks Davis, *The Evidential Force of Religious Experience* (Oxford: Clarendon Press, 1989); and William James, *The Varieties of Religious Experience: A Study in Human Nature* (New York: Collier Books, Macmillan, 1961).

9. I agree with Louis Dupré, who argues that a religious response to the problem of suffering requires a framework of theodicy which emphasizes a 'religious' versus a 'rationalist' understanding of God. When thinking about the problem of evil, many people, perhaps even Ivan in *The Brothers Karamazov*, tend to think of God as a Being distanced and separated in some deep sense from creation and humanity. This rationalist idea of God perhaps became most popularized in 'deism' of seventeenth-century England, by the writings of John Toland (*Christianity not Mysterious*) and Matthew Tindal (*Christianity as Old as the Creation*). However, typically in traditional 'religious' understandings, God is viewed theistically in intimate relationship with creation and humanity. God is primary Being from which everything has its existence and within which all is contained. God is omnipresent in creation and can and does act in and through the natural world.

Louis Dupré argues that it is this latter religious perspective – what he calls a 'Concrete-Religious' standpoint – that provides an inclusiveness to theology that takes into account elements of 'living faith', features that are typically neglected in rationalist–deistic critiques. How one views God is very significant in terms of how one understands the relevance of spiritual experience in responding to the problem of evil. Most importantly, it 'enables the Creator to share in the suffering of his creatures and thereby to redeem them'. It is from this kind of 'concrete, *theological* context', argues Dupré, that the believing philosopher is obliged to show that 'a belief in a good God is *compatible* with the existence of evil' (Dupré, 'Evil – A Religious Mystery', 261, 278). A rationalist–deistic framework, which radically separates God from creation, is not the view of God from which theologians need to respond to the problem of evil.

So the issue to which Dupré refers is one which exists at certain levels in Christian theology itself, rather than being a conflict solely between Christian theologians in general and atheistic sceptics. I suspect that deistic influences have penetrated deeply into much contemporary Christian thinking, so much so that some Christian theologians today work from an understanding of spiritual experience which rules out the possibility of any real human experience of intimate divine action. In this view spiritual experience is typically perceived as something wholly subjective, wherein God and spiritual realities are thought to be accessible to humankind solely as a human idea or feeling, disclosed in scriptural revelation or human inspiration, in the light of which human subjects interpret and integrate their everyday experiences.

On a similar line, in exploring the possibilities of divine healing of human suffering, Morton T. Kelsey writes critically of the prevalence in modern Christianity of a 'tacit acceptance, philosophically and theologically, of a world view which allows no place for a breakthrough of "divine" power into the space–time world. Such a breakthrough as healing is simply considered an impossibility.' Morton attributes this religious view of the world as a closed system originally to Aristotelian influences upon Christian theology. I suspect that the historical factors in this development might not be as straightforward as Morton suggests. However, I think he comments insightfully upon a Christian worldview, quite common today, of a 'closed rational and physical system', which God and spirits cannot or do not penetrate. Such a view severely limits one's initial openness to the possible healing that might occur through sacramental liturgy or other forms of prayer. Morton T. Kelsey, *Healing and Christianity: In Ancient Thought and Modern Times* (New York: Harper & Row, 1973), pp. 307–8, 309.

10. Alvin Plantinga suggests how it is logically possible to construe even what we traditionally regard as natural evil (evil which arises from the excesses and deficiencies of the natural world) in terms of the free-will defence, by attributing it to the misuse of freedom on the part of non-human spirits. *God, Freedom and Evil* (New York: Harper & Row, 1974), pp. 57–9.

11. This is an interpretation which in outline-structure is proposed by Nicolai Berdyaev, Erich Fromm, John Hick, G. W. F. Hegel, Carl Jung, Marjorie Hewitt Suchocki, and others. Also, there are interesting correspondences between this interpretation of the Fall myth and Julian of Norwich's vision of the parable of the servant in her *Revelation of Love*. In Julian's account, the Fall is to be construed as the external difficulties that a person experiences on a special errand for God, obstacles so severe that they very nearly overwhelm her or him on the journey. She writes: 'Then I looked close at him to see if I could perceive any fault, or if perhaps the lord would find any blame in him; but truly there was none to see. For it was only his own good will and great willingness that had caused his falling; and he was as keen and as inwardly well disposed as when he stood before his lord all ready to do his will. And even so his good lord continues to behold him with the same love and tenderness.' *Revelation of Love*, trans. John Skinner (New York: Image Books, 1997), p. 101; also see pp. 91, 96–9.

12. John Hick, *Evil and the God of Love*, rev. edn (New York: HarperSanFrancisco, 1977). Jane Mary Zwerner gives an interesting outline of Hick's view of 'soul-making', one that is drawn especially into reflections on Jesus' Passion and Resurrection which correspond to themes of this book. She writes: 'As Hick explains, the ultimate value is not happiness or health, though these are certainly good things which we rightly enjoy. Rather, the ultimate purpose of human existence is to attain personal moral and spiritual life, to realize the likeness of God. The death of Christ on the cross and his resurrection demonstrate that transfiguration can occur, and must occur, within the context of suffering.' 'The Discovery of Christian Meaning in Suffering: Transformation and Solidarity', *Evil and the Response of World Religions*, ed. William Cenkner (St Paul, MN: Paragon House, 1997), p. 45.

13. In correspondence.
14. James Wood, 'Twister', *The New Republic*, Vol. 218, No. 23 (June 8, 1998), 46.
15. William Blake, 'On Another's Sorrow', in *William Blake*, ed. J. Bronowski (New York: Viking Penguin, 1984), pp. 39–40.

2 Transformative Suffering

1. Dorothee Soelle, *Suffering*, trans. Everett R. Kalin (Philadelphia: Fortress Press, 1975), p. 124.
2. I have adapted this passage so that the language is gender inclusive, because it seems pretty clear that the sermon was intended for both 'sons' and 'daughters' of God within the Jewish–Christian community to which it was directed.
   This theme of transformative suffering is also proposed by some of the companions in the book of *Job*. Writing of it as 'divine discipline', Daniel Harrington discusses its development in *Proverbs*, *Sirach*, *2 Maccabees*, and, especially, *The Letter to the Hebrews*. See *Why Do We Suffer? A Scriptural Approach to the Human Condition* (Franklin, WI: Sheed & Ward, 2000), pp. 128–32. In his book Harrington also illuminates various other themes of or approaches to suffering given in Christian scripture, such as retribution, sacrifice and atonement, apocalyptism, and mystery.
3. Pamela A. Smith surveys writing by Elaine Scarry, Elisabeth Young-Bruehl, Edith Barfoot, Daniel Liderbach, and others, on the apparent correspondences between suffering and creativity. She notes, for example, that Paul Tournier 'insists that suffering can be "the occasion" which "gives rise" to suffering' (p. 184). Also, George Pickering observes how 'illness thus seems, in certain creative personalities, to have abetted their creative impulses in some causal way – and so to have been integral to their creativity' (p. 164). Pamela A. Smith, 'Chronic Pain and Creative Possibility: A Psychological Phenomenon Confronts Theologies of Suffering', in Maureen A. Tilley and Susan A. Ross (eds), *Broken and Whole: Essays on Religion and the Body* (Lanham, MD: University Press of America, 1995); Paul Tournier, *Creative Suffering*, trans. Edwin Hudson (New York: Harper & Row, 1982); George Pickering, *Creative Malady: Illness in the Lives and Minds of Charles Darwin, Florence Nightingale, Mary Baker Eddy, Sigmund Freud, Marcel Proust, Elizabeth Barrett Browning* (New York: Oxford University Press, 1974).
4. For studies concerning the various possible phenomena and contexts that cause suffering see, for example, Soelle, *Suffering*, Asenath Petri, *Individuality in Pain and Suffering*, 2nd edn (Chicago: University of Chicago Press, 1978), and Eric J. Cassel, 'The Nature of Suffering and the Goals of Medicine', *New England Journal of Medicine*, Vol. 306 (1982), 639–45.
5. John Hick, *Evil and the God of Love*, rev. edn (New York: HarperSanFrancisco, 1977), p. 318. The distinction between physical and psychic pain that I am making here is outlined by Hick on pp. 292–320. See a similar definition explored by Eric J. Cassel, in 'The Nature of Suffering and the Goals of Medicine', especially p. 641.
6. For two helpful overviews and analyses of various definitions of spirituality, see Walter Principe, 'Toward Defining Spirituality', *Studies in Religion*,

Vol. 12, (1983), 127–41, and Sandra M. Schneiders, 'Spirituality in the Academy', *Theological Studies*, Vol. 50 (1989), 676–97.
7. John Hick, *Evil and the God of Love*, pp. 382–3.
8. See Lawrence S. Cunningham and Keith J. Egan, *Christian Spirituality: Themes from the Tradition* (New York: Paulist Press, 1996), pp. 5–28, which focuses upon specifically 'Christian' elements in defining spirituality. A Christian spirituality is a Christ-centred spirituality that includes both transcendent and immanent senses of a Trinitarian God. The Christian life-orientation involves the ideas of a graced conversion and vocation of discipleship that embraces the whole of the person, focuses on community and history, and finds its spiritual nourishment in various practices, with emphasis on eucharistic sharing.
9. Depending on the region of habitation, dialect, and/or anthropologist in question, the Bushmen are called a variety of different names. Common names are the 'Kung', 'Basarwa', 'Kua', and 'San' people. For an interesting and scholarly account of essential attitudes, beliefs, and practices of the Kua, including comparative analyses of these with other groups of Bushmen, see Carlos Valiente-Noailles, *The Kua: Life and Soul of the Central Kalahari Bushmen* (Rotterdam: A. A. Balkema, 1993).

   For the Kung and other groups of Bushmen, the traditional hunting and gathering lifestyle is presently under intense pressures from agricultural expansion into their traditional lands and the decline of game. Attempts at integration into western economic and industrialized modes of living and working have led to conditions of poverty, unemployment, racial persecution, and alcoholism. Although there is some resistance to integration, it appears doubtful that the Kung will be able to continue many of their traditional ways of life. See for example, 'Botswana Is Pressing Bushmen to Leave Reserve', *The New York Times* (14 July 1996) I, 3; 1, and 'The Bushmen's Advocate', *The Washington Post* (18 December 1995) D, 1; 4.
10. Richard Katz, *Boiling Energy: Community Healing among the Kalahari Kung* (Cambridge, MA: Harvard University Press, 1982), p. 45.
11. Ibid., pp. 97, 134.
12. Ibid., p. 245.
13. Ibid., p. 194.
14. Kilton Stewart, *Pygmies and Dream Giants* (New York: Harper Colophon Books, 1975), pp. 46, 47.
15. Ibid., p. 47.
16. Contemporary demonology tends to distinguish between various levels or degrees of spirit contact: terms such as 'obsession', 'oppression', 'infestation', and 'affliction' indicate different stages, where a person is affected in various ways and degrees by an evil spirit. 'Possession' marks a complete infiltration and domination of the personality by a spirit. Regarding its current popularity, Michael Cuneo estimates conservatively that 'there are at least five or six hundred evangelical exorcism ministries in operation today [in the United States], and quite possibly two or three times this many.' Michael W. Cuneo, *American Exorcism: Expelling Demons in the Land of Plenty* (New York: Doubleday, 2001), p. 209.
17. See, for example, M. Scott Peck, *People of the Lie: The Hope for Healing Human Evil* (New York: Simon & Schuster, 1983) and Donald Evans, *Spirituality and*

Human Nature (Albany, NY: SUNY Press, 1993). Also, the theme is developed in even more controversial ways throughout many of the works of Omraam Mikhaël Aïvanhov. A brief example is 'Unwanted Guests', in *Life Force*, Vol. 5 of *Complete Works* (Fréjus, France: Prosveta, 1993), pp. 153–68.

18. Morton T. Kelsey, *Healing and Christianity: In Ancient Thought and Modern Times* (New York: Harper & Row, 1973), p. 294.
19. Cuneo, *American Exorcism*, p. 162. See also p. 152. Cuneo's book is an informative and entertaining overview of the belief in and practice of demonic and satanic exorcisms and deliverances. It includes reference to a variety of Christian denominations from over the last 50 years or so. Although its style and tone are rather informal and conversational, the book is an impressive contemporary history and cultural commentary on the phenomena. Other influential and controversial books on the subject are: Malachi Martin, *Hostage to the Devil* (New York: Reader's Digest/Thomas Y. Crowell, 1976); Francis McNutt, *Healing* (Altamonte Springs, FL: Creation House, 1988); M. Scott Peck, *People of the Lie*. See Cuneo also for various other relevant sources.
20. See, for example, Larry Dossy, 'The Return of Prayer', *Alternative Therapies*, Vol. 3, No. 6 (November 1997), 10–17, 113–20. In this article Dossy clarifies various methodological considerations and theoretical issues related to prayer. He acknowledges the significance of 'empathy, caring, and compassion' (p. 113) in intercessory prayer and he cites a number of studies and sources which support the efficacy of healing prayer and distant mental intentionality. Perhaps most significant is the collection he cites by Daniel J. Benor, *Healing Research*, Vols 1–4 (Munich, Germany: Helix, 1993).
21. Edith Stein, *On the Problem of Empathy*, trans. Waltraut Stein, 3rd rev. edn, Vol. 3 of *The Collected Works of Edith Stein* (Washington, DC: ICS Publications, 1989), pp. 11, 10.
22. Ibid., pp. 23, 14.
23. John E. Nelson, *Healing the Split: Integrating Spirit into Our Understanding of the Mentally Ill*, rev. ed (Albany, NY: SUNY Press, 1994), p. 386.
24. Viktor Frankl, *Man's Search for Meaning: An Introduction to Logotherapy*, 4th edn (Boston: Beacon Press, 1992), pp. 81, 80.
25. Ibid., p. 115. Frankl's sufferings became challenges for him to explore and confirm the psycho-dynamics of the human spirit within conditions of extreme deprivation. His struggles to find meaning in his suffering are the foundation of the psychoanalytic school of 'logotherapy'. Following the War, Frankl goes on further to develop and practice a theory of psychology around what he claims is a fundamental human drive for meaning. Frankl had formally articulated this view of logotherapy before the War, by 1937, and it had originated in the mid 1920s. In *Man's Search for Meaning* (written originally in 1946 as *Was nicht in meinen Büchern steht*) he refers to his concentration camp experiences to illustrate logotherapy and to justify its claims.

Some critics argue that Frankl's work is perverse in the way that it misrepresents the destructive nature of the Holocaust. Supporting and extending the scathing criticisms by Lawrence Langer, Timothy Pytell writes that 'Frankl's emphasis on stoic and heroic suffering in effect obscures the nihilistic evil of the Holocaust. In order to still the pain of loss and guilt, he constructed a narrative of meaning.' See Timothy E. Pytell, 'Redeeming the

Unredeemable: Auschwitz and *Man's Search for Meaning*', *Holocaust and Genocide Studies*, Vol. 17 (2003), 90–1, 103; and Lawrence Langer, 'The Literature of Auschwitz', in *Anatomy of the Auschwitz Death Camp*, ed. Yisrael Gutman and Michael Berenbaum (Bloomington: Indiana University Press and the US Holocaust Museum, 1994). My thanks to Jeanette Unger, for bringing these sources to my attention.

Despite these concerns, Frankl would no doubt argue that at least some of his suffering in Auschwitz contributed positively to his own spiritual life-orientation and his later professional work. I suspect the difficulties and controversies surrounding Frankl's views arise from the fact that he does not acknowledge the reality of destructive suffering alongside that of transformative suffering. He did not know how to fit destructive suffering within his theological and psychological frameworks. Therefore in his writings he cannot really respond effectively and compassionately to the many victims who are destroyed by their suffering in the camps. See Chapter 4, which focuses on destructive suffering.

26. Rainer Maria Rilke, *Letters To A Young Poet*, trans. Stephen Mitchell (New York: Vintage Books, 1984), pp. 68–9.
27. Soelle, *Suffering*, p. 127.
28. Ibid., p. 125. Also, Jane Mary Zwerner observes: 'Suffering instructs and transforms for it confronts persons with their limitations and dependencies upon God and other persons. Many insights, for example, patience, tolerance, compassion and mercy, are most truly revealed within the context of great personal loss.' 'The Discovery of Christian Meaning in Suffering: Transformation and Solidarity', *Evil and the Response of World Religion*, ed. William Cenkner (St Paul, MI: Paragon House, 1997), p. 49.

See also Eric J. Cassel's exploration of various positive effects of certain kinds of suffering in 'The Nature of Suffering and the Goals of Medicine', especially 643–4; and for a recent psychological exploration of 'the effect of ritual pain on consciousness and identity', see Ariel Glucklich, *Sacred Pain: Hurting the Body for the Sake of the Soul* (New York: Oxford University Press, 2001), p. 8.

29. Pope John Paul II also writes: 'What we express by the word "suffering" seems to be particularly *essential to the nature of man*. It is as deep as man himself, precisely because it manifests in its own way that depth which is proper to man, and in its own way surpasses it.' 'Suffering is also an invitation to manifest the moral greatness of man, his *spiritual maturity*.' *On the Christian Meaning of Human Suffering* (Boston, MA: St Paul Books & Media, 1984), pp. 6, 35.
30. Nelson, *Healing the Split*, p. 261.
31. Oliver Davies, *A Theology of Compassion: Metaphysics of Difference and the Renewal of Tradition* (Cambridge, MA: William B. Eerdmans, 2001), p. 18, in reference to Martha Nussbaum, 'Compassion: The Basic Social Emotion', *Social Philosophy and Policy*, Vol. 13 (1996), 27–58.

Drawing on Aristotle, Nussbaum also argues that in order for one to feel compassion towards another person the suffering of that person needs to be significant and not trivial, the person who is suffering cannot be regarded as primarily culpable and blamed for the suffering, and one needs to be able to imagine oneself suffering in similar circumstances (pp. 31–8).

Davies focuses more in his book on the dynamics of compassion for the agent, rather than its effect on the receiver. He wants to show how compassion reveals the dynamics 'of consciousness itself, and thus provides a resource for articulating a new language of being' (p. 20). His book is a creative exploration of the theological significance of this 'language of being,' as it is revealed through the structure of compassion. In introductory summary he writes: 'The assumption of another's suffering as one's own entails a radical decentring of the self, and a putting at risk of the self, in the free re-enactment of the dispossessed state of those who suffer. Compassion is the recognition of the otherness of the other, as an otherness which stands beyond our own world, beyond our own constructions of otherness even. But it is also the discovery of our own nature, as a horizon of subjectivity which is foundationally ordered to the world of another's experience... It is here then, in the dispossessive act whereby the self assumes the burdens of the other, and thus accepts the surplus of its own identity, that we should recognise the veiled presence of being' (p. 17).

I am focusing more in my book on how the structure of compassion reveals a shared intimacy with the sufferer and provides an active healing power of love.

32. Davies, *A Theology of Compassion*, p. 18.
33. Donald Evans writes: 'A few years ago at a theological conference I heard a paper in which a scholar said something like this, "And St Paul, following the traditional metaphor already used by Jeremiah and Ezekiel, spoke of a spirit of love dwelling in the heart." As I heard these words I wanted to jump to my feet and protest: "Surely it's possible that St Paul spoke of a spirit of love dwelling in the heart because that's where he *experienced* it – as countless others have in many different religious traditions. It's no metaphor, it's a literal truth."' 'Can Philosophers Limit What Mystics Can Do? A Critique of Steven Katz', *Religious Studies*, 25 (1989), 59.
34. Developing out of Hindu and Buddhist traditions, chakras are thought to be vortices of psychic and spiritual forces of the subtle body that are normally unconscious and constricted or knotted within the human person. Through appropriate religious practices and surrender, they can be opened, expanded, and integrated with the physical body, thus bringing to consciousness the energies, emotions, abilities, knowledge, and spiritual realities associated with them. They are located around the following areas of the physical body: the base of the spine, pelvis, naval, heart, larynx, and the centres of the lower forehead and the crown at the top of the head (though the crown centre is not traditionally regarded as a chakra because it is located above the body).

Hindu and Christian theories of these energy centres or chakras help in understanding the possible spiritual dynamics of compassion and also in interpreting the healing dynamics of the Kung people described in this chapter. A vividly illustrated introduction to the chakras is Ajit Mookerjee, *Kundalini: The Arousal of the Inner Energy* (Rochester, NY: Destiny Books, 1991). The clearest and most rigorous account that I have read is the early twentieth-century work of Sir John Woodroffe (Arthur Avalon). See *The Serpent Power*, 9th edn (New York: Dover, 1974) and *Introduction to Tantra Śāstra*, 4th edn (Madras: Ganesh, 1963).

35. This anonymous Christian Hermeticist draws the chakras into his spirituality in qualified ways, stressing the penultimate significance of the heart centre in Christian spirituality. Anonymous, *Meditations on the Tarot: A Journey into Christian Hermeticism*, trans. Robert A. Powell (Rockport MA: Element, 1985), p. 227.
36. Carl Jung, *Memories, Dreams, Reflections by C.G. Jung*, ed. Amiela Jaffe, trans. Richard and Clara Winston (New York: Vintage Books, 1963), p. 134.
37. Kelsey, *Healing and Christianity*, p. 57. Kelsey points out that almost one-fifth of the Gospel narratives pertain to the healing activities of Jesus (p. 54). John P. Meier notes that in the Gospel of Mark the reference to miracles constitutes 31 per cent of the total 666 verses and 47 per cent of the public ministry narrative. This is a great deal of attention given to the subject. Maier discusses how favourably this material fares under the analysis of contemporary biblical criticism, providing strong support for the historical authenticity of at least a significant number of healing miracles. These criteria include: multiple attestation from various sources and forms; coherence and consistency in description and interpretation; dissimilarity to miracle narratives from other sources; embarrassment about what was being said about Jesus; and the depth of detail that is given surrounding various events. In light of the textual evidence, especially on the support of the criteria of multiple attestation and coherence, Meier concludes that it is a 'historical fact that Jesus performed extraordinary deeds deemed by himself and others to be miracles'. John P. Meier, *A Marginal Jew: Rethinking the Historical Jesus*, Vol. II, *Mentor, Message, and Miracle* (New York: Anchor Bible Reference Library, Doubleday, 1994), pp. 619, 630.
38. Michael Harner, *The Way of the Shaman* (San Francisco: Harper & Row, 1990), p. xiv. As quoted in Nelson, *Healing the Split*, pp. 394–5.
39. Henri J. M. Nouwen, *The Wounded Healer* (Toronto: Image Books, Doubleday, 1979), pp. 82–3. This book is a popular pastoral exploration of the theme of the wounded healer in Christian theology.
40. Anonymous, *Meditations on the Tarot*, pp. 80–1.
41. Soelle, *Suffering*, pp. 139–40.

3 Suffering and Christ

1. William Blake, 'On Another's Sorrow,' in *William Blake*, ed. J. Bronowski (New York: Viking Penguin, 1958), pp. 39–40.
2. Morton T. Kelsey, *Healing and Christianity: In Ancient Thought and Modern Times* (New York: Harper & Row, 1973), p. 67.
3. Marcus Borg, *Meeting Jesus Again for the First Time: The Historical Jesus and the Heart of Contemporary Faith* (New York: HarperSanFrancisco, 1994) p. 61.
4. Dorothee Soelle, *Suffering*, trans. Everett R. Kalin (Philadelphia: Fortress Press, 1975), p. 36.
5. Fyodor Dostoevsky, *The Brothers Karamazov*, the Garnett translation, revised by Ralph E. Matlaw (New York: W. W. Norton, 1976), p. 222.
6. In line with my development of the nature of empathy in Chapter 2, Marjorie Hewitt Suchocki notes how self-transcendence is associated with empathy. 'Empathy... involves recognition of the other as subjective other

in relation to the self. Empathy is the de-absolutization of the self and therefore the transcendence of the self by knowing the self as one center among many centers, participating in a universe of centerless centering. Empathy requires a "feeling-with" that mediates the sense of interconnectedness...' I would add how the self-transcendence that occurs in empathy is not necessarily positive or constructive: it will be contexualized either masochistically, sadistically, or compassionately. *The Fall to Violence: Original Sin in Relational Theology* (New York: Continuum, 1994), p. 147.
7. Borg, *Meeting Jesus Again for the First Time*, p. 60.
8. Ibid., Martha Nussbaum also calls for a politics of compassion, stressing the possible significance of compassion in contemporary public life. Moral critics of compassion, such as the ancient Stoics, Immanuel Kant, and Friedrich Nietzsche, depict it as a narrowing and biased subjective emotion that is irrational and alien to a healthy ethical orientation grounded in objective reason. Against that view, Nussbaum shows how compassion involves a certain kind of rational 'thought about the well being of others' (p. 28). In its connection with and concern for the suffering of others, compassion functions rationally as a social emotion that motivates people ethically. From this basis Professor Nussbaum goes on to argue that compassion ought to play a significant role in economic planning, legal reasoning and the structure of public institutions, such as welfare and taxation systems. She advocates that 'public education at every level should cultivate the ability to imagine the experiences of others and to participate in their sufferings' (p. 50) and that one 'should demand political leaders who display the abilities involved in compassion' (p. 51). Martha Nussbaum, 'Compassion: The Basic Social Emotion', *Social Philosophy and Policy*, Vol. 13 (1996), 27–58.
9. See, for example, the papal letters: Pope John Paul II, *On Human Work: Laborem Exercens* (Boston: Daughters of St Paul, 1981) and Pope Leo XIII, *On the Condition of the Working Class: Rerum Novarum* (Boston: Pauline Books & Media, 2000); and a document from the Second Vatican Council: Pope Paul VI, *Pastoral Constitution of the Church in the Modern World: Gaudium et Spes* (Boston: Pauline Books & Media, 1965). For other related material on Roman Catholic social teaching see David O'Brien and Thomas A. Shannon (eds), *Catholic Social Thought: The Documentary Heritage* (Maryknoll, NY: Orbis Books, 1992).
10. Dorothee Soelle with Shirley A. Cloyes, *To Work and To Love: A Theology of Creation* (Philadelphia: Fortress Press, 1984), especially pp. 83–92.
11. Soelle, *To Work and To Love*, p. 89.
12. Pope John Paul II, *On Human Work: Laborem Exercens*, p. 23.
13. See for example Gustavo Gutiérrez, *A Theology of Liberation: History, Politics, and Salvation*, rev. edn, trans. Caridad Inda and John Eagleson (Maryknoll, NY: Orbis Books, 1988).

Another significant social justice movement within the Roman Catholic Church is 'The Catholic Worker'. It was established in 1933 by two lay Catholics, Dorothy Day and Peter Maurin. For an outline and brief history of the movement see Dorothy Day, *The Long Loneliness: The Autobiography of Dorothy Day* (New York: HarperSanFrancisco, 1997). The Catholic Worker and Liberation theologians share similar orientations: both focus in their theology and ministry on the poor, unemployed, homeless and exploited people; both stress a theology of praxis that emphasizes social theory and action; and both draw on the critiques of social theorists from outside of the Church in support of their views.

14. See for example Elizabeth A. Johnson, *She Who Is: The Mystery of God in Feminist Theological Discourse* (New York: Crossroad, 2002) and Sally McFague, *Models of God* (Philadelphia: Fortress Press, 1987). For more radical feminist critiques and theologies see: Mary Daly, *Beyond God the Father* (Boston: Beacon Press, 1973); and Grace Jantzen, *Power, Gender and Christian Mysticism* (Cambridge: Cambridge University Press, 1995), and *Becoming Divine: Towards a Feminist Philosophy of Religion* (Bloomington, IN: Indiana University Press, 1999).

15. Lynn White, Jr, 'The Historical Roots of our Ecological Crisis', *Science*, Vol. 155, No. 3767 (10 March 1967), as reprinted in *The Christian Difference* (Needham Heights, MA: Pearson Custom, 1999), p. 406.

16. Ibid., pp. 404–5. White cites a provocative example. 'A Governor of California, like myself a churchman but less troubled than I, spoke for the Christian tradition when he said (as is alleged), "When you've seen one redwood tree, you've seen them all." To a Christian a tree can be no more than a physical fact. The whole concept of a sacred grove is alien to Christianity and to the ethos of the west' (pp. 406–7).

I have a related story. A few years ago, Chris McDonald introduced me and some friends to a small stand of old growth white pine trees in Algonquin Park in Ontario. I had not seen a group of these trees before. We could access them only via canoe and portage, through four lakes. I suspect they were left there by accident, overlooked in the cutting of the forest, which years ago had cleared almost all of the natural growth in the province. Although these trees are not of the stature of California redwoods, they are quite large, beautiful and magnificent, especially relative to current standards of growth in Ontario. They can grow to over 45 metres and live for over 400 years, withstanding the extremes of forest fires and the cold Canadian winters. Two centuries ago, white pines were the dominant trees in Ontario. In contrast to current forest in the Park, these trees have a definite majesty and a spiritual energy that is remarkable and quite palpable, even for those of us who are not very sensitive to nature. It is amazing to me how our Canadian forefathers, in their zeal to harvest the vast resources of our land, did not think and plan to leave even a small number of accessible stands of these amazing trees, for their descendents to enjoy, appreciate, and honour.

17. Ibid., p. 408.

18. Edith Stein, *Finite and Eternal Being: An Attempt at an Ascent To the Meaning of Being*, trans. Kurt F. Reinhardt, Vol. 9 of *The Collected Works of Edith Stein*, ed. L. Gelber and Romaeus Leuven, OCD (Washington, DC: ICS Publications, 2002), p. 423.

19. Marian Maskulak, *Reclaiming the Soul: Edith Stein and the Unity of the Body–Soul–Spirit at the Center of Holistic Formation*, PhD thesis (Regis College, forthcoming, 2005), p. 93. Maskulak's quote from Stein is her own translation of Edith Stein, *Der Aufbau der menschlichen Person*, rev. edn, ed. Beate Beckmann-Zöller, Vol. 14 of *Edith Stein Gesamtausgabe*, Klaus Mass and Hanna-Barbara Gerl-Falkovitz (Freiburg: Herder, 2004), p. 115.

20. Lynn White, Jr, 'The Historical Roots', in *The Christian Difference*, p. 408.
21. See for example: Thomas Berry et. al., *Befriending the Earth: A Theology of Reconciliation between Humans and the Earth* (Mystic, CT: Twenty-Third Publications, 1991); Thomas Berry, *The Dream of the Earth* (San Francisco: Sierra Club Books, 1988); and Eleazar S. Fernandez, *Reimagining the Human: Theological Anthropology in Response to Systemic Evil* (St Louis, MO: Chalice Press, 2004). Also, in *The Fall to Violence*, Marjorie Hewitt Suchocki develops an interesting process theology on this perspective, in proposing what she calls a 'relational theology' that re-appropriates 'the ancient doctrine of original sin, albeit in a relational world where its fundamental nature is measured by the degree to which it contributes to unnecessary violence against creation' (p. 14). In exploring various complex webs of interconnectedness between all of the phenomena of creation, she stresses 'reciprocal relations of well-being'. These relations entail responsibility, solidarity, and mutual caring amongst humanity and in relation to the environment (pp. 70, 42).
22. Louis Dupré, 'Evil – A Religious Mystery: A Plea for a More Inclusive Model of Theodicy,' *Faith and Philosophy*, Vol. 7 (1990), 274.
23. Soelle, *Suffering*, p. 125.
24. Ibid., pp. 21–2.
25. Morton Kelsey writes, 'The "Christian" attitude that glories in sickness is completely alien to that of Jesus of Nazareth; it is aligned on the side of what he was fighting against. I very much suspect that anyone who glories in the benefits of illness has either known little of it in himself or those dear to him, or else has serious masochistic tendencies. Sickness is a destructive and evil phenomenon, and Christ as the incarnation of creativity was dead set against it.' *Healing and Christianity*, p. 90.
26. Dermot A. Lane, *Keeping Hope Alive: Stirrings in Christian Theology* (New York: Paulist Press, 1996), p. 71.
27. Soelle, *Suffering*, pp. 139–40. On this theme Dermot Lane writes: 'I submit that the God revealed in the life and death of Jesus is analogically speaking "a suffering God" and that this same God continues to suffer in the world until God comes again. The God revealed in Jesus is a God who affects the world and continues to be affected by the suffering of the world. The proposal of "a suffering God" of course does not eliminate the problem of human suffering but it does give us a way of facing suffering in the knowledge that we do not suffer alone but with God as the fellow-sufferer who understands.' *Keeping Hope Alive*, p. 71. This theme is also developed in his book *Christ at the Centre: Selected Issues in Christology* (Dublin: Veritas, 1990), pp. 53–79. Also, for context surrounding the 'modern refusal to take the route of merely humanizing the sufferings of Christ', see Paul S. Fiddes, *The Creative Suffering of God* (Oxford: Clarendon Press, 1988), especially pp. 25–31.

The point I wish to stress here is that for some Christians it is not merely the *idea* of a suffering God that heals and consoles but the *actual presence* of the compassionate Christ that is felt by the believer. Henri Le Saux (Abhishiktānanda), a modern Benedictine monk and theologian who was involved in Hindu–Christian dialogue, stresses both the present significance of Jesus' Passion and Resurrection and the human experience of His real

presence: 'Jesus is at the same time the one who is seated in peace and glory at the Father's right hand, and the one whose Passion is continued in his members until the end of the world. Good Friday is the remembrance, together with the Passion of Jesus, of all the poor (*anāwīm*) of all times and places, crushed by their fellow men, and culminating in the Passion of Jesus.' 'Jesus lived and died. That belongs to the past. What is Real is that he lives as "risen". It is as risen that we must meet him, not in memory. Risen and having recovered the glory that was his in the beginning; the one in whom, for whom, by whom, everything was made, the one in whom everything is established.' Abhishiktānanda, *Ascent to the Depth of the Heart: The Spiritual Diary (1948–1973) of Swāmī Abhishiktānanda (Dom H. Le Saux)*, A selection, edited with introduction and notes, by Raimon Panikkar, translated by David Fleming and James Stuart (Delhi: ISPCK, 1998), pp. 241, 257. For a good overview of Henri Le Saux's life and teaching see James A. Wiseman, '"Enveloped by Mystery": The Spiritual Journey of Henri Le Saux/Abhishiktānanda,' *Église et Théologie*, Vol. 23 (1992), 241–60.
28. Charles B. Guignon (ed), *Dostoevsky: The Grand Inquisitor*, with related chapters from *The Brothers Karamazov* (Indianapolis: Hackett, 1993), pp. xxxvii–xxxviii.
29. Soelle, *Suffering*, p. 124.
30. Ibid., p. 127.
31. Dostoevsky, *The Brothers Karamazov*, p. 282.
32. Ibid., pp. 282, 295, 297.
33. Ibid., pp. 226–7.
34. Soelle, *Suffering*, p. 92.
35. David N. Power, 'Sacrament: Event Eventing', in *A Promise of Presence*, ed. Michael Downey and Richard Fragomeni (Washington, DC: Pastoral Press, 1992), pp. 288, 292, 293.
36. Henri J. M. Nouwen, Donald P. McNeill and Douglas A. Morrison, *Compassion: A Reflection on the Christian Life* (Toronto: Image Book, Doubleday, 1983), p. 52.
37. Ibid.
38. From a letter of Henri Le Saux (Abhishiktānanda) to Marc Chaduc, 8 April 1973, in *Swāmī Abhishiktānanda: His Life Told through His Letters* ed. and trans. James Stuart (Delhi: ISPCK, 1989), p. 328. In the revised edition (ISPCK, 1995) the quote is on p. 292.
39. Dostoevksy, *The Brothers Karamazov*, 298.
40. Matthew Fox (ed and comm), *Breakthrough: Meister Eckhart's Creation Spirituality in New Translation* (New York: Image Books, 1980), p. 234, as quoted from Meister Eckhart, *Meister Eckhart: Selected Treatises and Sermons Translated from Latin and German with an Introduction and Notes*, ed. James Clark and John V. Skinner (London, Faber & Faber, 1958), p. 115.
41. Dupré, 'Evil – A Religious Mystery', 278.
42. Pope John Paul II, *On the Christian Meaning of Human Suffering* (Boston: St Paul Books & Media, 1984), p. 45.
43. Thomas Merton, *New Seeds of Contemplation* (New York: New Directions Books, 1972), p. 5.
44. Ibid., p. 3.

45. Ibid., p. 5.
46. Julian of Norwich, *Revelation of Love*, trans. John Skinner (New York: Image Books, 1996), pp. 39, 42. See also especially pp. 38–9.
47. See Grace Jantzen, *Julian of Norwich: Mystic and Theologian* (New York: Paulist Press, 1988), pp. 149–61.
48. Julian of Norwich, *Revelation of Love*, p. 134.
49. Ibid.
50. Michael Ivens, *Understanding the Spiritual Exercises: Text and Commentary, A Handbook for Retreat Directors* (Leominster, Herefordshire: Gracewing, 1998), p. 147.
51. Eckhart, *Meister Eckhart: Teacher and Preacher*, ed. Bernard McGinn, trans. Frank Tobin (New York: Paulist Press, 1986), p. 330.
52. Eckhart, *Meister Eckhart: Selected Treatises and Sermons*, ed. Clark and Skinner p. 142.
53. Michael Harner, *The Way of the Shaman* (San Francisco: Harper & Row, 1990), p. xiv, as quoted in John E. Nelson, *Healing the Split: Integrating Spirit Into Our Understanding of the Mentally Ill*, rev edn (Albany, NY: SUNY Press, 1994), pp. 394–5.
54. Soelle, *Suffering*, p. 155.
55. Evelyn Underhill, *Fragments from an Inner Life*, ed. Dana Greene (Harrisburg, PA: Morehouse, 1993), p. 63.
56. Fox, *Breakthrough*, p. 235.
57. Soelle, *Suffering*, pp. 96, 95 and 98.
58. Fox, *Breakthrough*, pp. 276–7. Marilyn McCord Adams shows how this consciousness can be understood as a compensatory consolation for the sufferings one experiences in life. See 'Redemptive Suffering: A Christian Solution to the Problem of Evil', *Rationality, Religious Belief, and Moral Commitment: New Essays in the Philosophy of Religion*, ed. Robert Audi and William Wainwright (Ithaca: Cornell University Press, 1986), pp. 248–67.

    However, Eleanor Stump poses the criticism raised against approaches in theodicy which stress Christian consolation: 'although the evil is compensated, it isn't integrated into the Christian story of the sufferer's life. Because suffering isn't any way necessary to the good that compensates it, we might wonder why God doesn't simply grant human beings the experience of union with Christ without allowing them to suffer first.' 'Aquinas on the Sufferings of Job', *Reasoned Faith: Essays in Philosophical Theology in Honour of Norman Kretzmann*, ed. Eleanor Stump (Ithaca, NY: Cornell University Press, 1993), pp. 330–1, especially note 9.

    The focus in my book is not on the compensation that Christianity offers to *make up* for past suffering, but on the possibly transformative nature of suffering and the integration of it into a consciousness of love. In this way, in answer to Stump's concerns, suffering is directly related to necessary conditions of the ideal and the very compensation itself. And although some spiritual consolation does take the form of redemptive healing of the victims of destructive suffering, as we will see also in Chapter 4, this is not compensation for suffering but it enables the individual to continue her or his transformative journey towards surrender and union with God and the embodiment of the Divine.

59. Dermot Lane describes this process as the 'creative paradox' of Christian conversion: 'It is normative in terms of summing up the meaning and structure of salvation, and paradigmatic in terms of the process required for becoming part of the *Eschaton* already established in Christ. Contact with the crucified and risen Christ, becoming a disciple, involves a personal process of dying and rising, of passing over into Christ, a movement of decentring the self in order to recentre the self in Christ.' *Keeping Hope Alive*, p. 114.
60. Dostoevsky, *The Brothers Karamazov*, pp. 299, 301.
61. Guignon, *Dostoevsky*, p. xlii.
62. Dostoevksy, *The Brothers Karamazov*, p. 298.
63. Soelle, *Suffering*, p. 91.
64. Fox, *Breakthrough*, p. 485.
65. See also Michael Stoeber, *Evil and the Mystics' God: Towards a Mystical Theodicy* (London: Macmillan, 1992) for an exploration of the significance of mystical experience in support of teleological theodicy. See especially Chapters 7 and 8, and an interpretative account of Dostoevsky's critique of theodicy in Chapter 2.

4 Destructive Suffering

1. Marilyn McCord Adams, *Horrendous Evils and the Goodness of God* (Ithaca, NY: Cornell University Press, 1999), pp. 26–7. In my view some destructive suffering is so devastating that it might constitute for the victim reason to question the overall goodness of his or her life. However, some destructive suffering is relatively minor and not that serious, though its effects remain negative for the victim. In this view, destructive suffering never itself contributes to a positive context or outcome for the victim.

    Adams supposes that horrendous suffering will in an afterlife context 'not only be balanced off but endowed with positive meanings, meanings at least some of which will be appropriated by the participant him/herself'. She speculates how such suffering might act to stimulate in the victim an openness to a mystical intimacy with God and that it is somehow possibly even itself 'a vision into the inner life of God' (pp. 205, 162, 161). Her view is influenced somewhat by a creative interpretation of the writings of Simone Weil by Diogenes Allen, in 'Natural Evil and the Love of God', *Religious Studies*, Vol. 16 (1980), 439–56. This essay is also in *The Problem of Evil*, Marilyn McCord Adams and Robert Merrihew Adams (Oxford: Oxford University Press, 1990), pp. 189–208.

    See also endnotes 2 and 26 in this chapter.
2. See especially Simone Weil, 'On the Love of God and Affliction', in *Simone Weil*, trans. Eric O. Springsted (Maryknoll, NY: Orbis Books, 1998), pp. 41–70. Affliction, for Weil, is very extreme physical, emotional and social suffering that is unjustified. Weil describes the absurdity of affliction, how such extreme, innocent suffering penetrates to the depths of one's being and how in such isolating distress one is unable to be open to God or even unable to love at all. Drawing on Platonic and Stoic sources, she grounds this affliction in the 'necessity' of regular mechanistic forces of matter,

which, though they are within divine providence, are separated from divine goodness and love. 'A blind mechanism, heedless of degrees of spiritual perfection, continually buffets men hither and thither and flings some of them at the very foot of the Cross' (p. 47). Weil urges one to hope and struggle to love from within this condition of affliction, and writes of the ability to consent or surrender 'to a right orientation' towards God (p. 55), even in such desolation: 'Whenever we have some pain to endure, we can [then] say to ourselves that it is the universe, the order and beauty of the world, and the obedience of creation to God which are entering our body' (p. 52).

By maintaining this positive stance while in affliction, one might help to centre oneself in God, from which affliction loses its devastating effects and is reduced. Weil writes of God's power to heal the victims of affliction, even if they will always be scarred by its effects (pp. 46, 52). She stresses especially the spiritual power of Christ in that regard, for he has experienced affliction in its fullness (pp. 66–7), and she speaks in other writings of her own experience of Christ's love in her suffering. She suggests that through this horrible struggle with affliction, one may eventually come to recognize 'things and events, everywhere and always', including this brutal necessity, 'as vibrations of the same divine and infinitely sweet word' (p. 52). Nevertheless, she insists adamantly, 'affliction is not [transformative] suffering. Affliction is something quite different from a divine educational method' (p. 53).

In a creative and insightful reading of Simone Weil's development of affliction, Diogenes Allen notes the stress in Weil on humbly surrendering to God in such affliction, using 'nature' as the provocative exemplar, in the way the processes of the natural world mechanically and unquestioningly follow the will of God. He interprets her account as suggesting that this radical suffering is a disguised form of God's love to which one needs to surrender. It is 'an indirect contact with a loving Father', where one 'is to find the distress itself as the touch of his love'. 'Natural Evil and the Love of God', pp. 452, 450.

Such an interpretation is quite different from suggesting only that a person might be healed by God despite her or his affliction, if she or he remains open to God's love, as I suggested above. The danger of Allen's interpretation of affliction is that it tends towards reducing the true horror of affliction by regarding it as instrumentally good (hence transformative suffering), in suggesting that it contributes to this positive experience of God or even that it actually is a positive experience of God. I suspect Weil would resist treating affliction as an instrumental good in this way, as I noted above, though perhaps there are passages of her writing that might be so interpreted.

I should note also that Weil's idea of 'necessity' within the divine creative action seems to correspond in interesting ways to Jacob Boehme's idea of the first principle of the Divine Essence, which in itself is a blind and amoral creative principle that provides the source for the vital dynamism of life. For a discussion of the significance of the first principle of the Divine Essence for theodicy, see Michael Stoeber, *Evil and the Mystics' God: Towards a Mystical Theodicy* (Toronto: University of Toronto Press, 1992), especially pp. 143–64.

3. *The Concise Oxford Dictionary*, 7th edn (Oxford: Oxford University Press, 1982), p. 260.
4. Dorothee Soelle, *Suffering*, trans. Everett R. Kalin (Philadelphia: Fortress Press, 1975), p. 91.
5. Tilley, *The Evils of Theodicy* (Washington, DC: Georgetown University Press, 1991), p. 235.
6. Grace Jantzen, *Becoming Divine: Towards a Feminist Philosophy of Religion* (Bloomington, Indiana: Indiana University Press, 1999), p. 259.
7. Ibid., p. 21.
8. Ibid., p. 260.
9. Ibid., pp. 261, 262.
10. Ibid., p. 263.
11. Ibid., p. 264.
12. Kenneth Surin, *Theology and the Problem of Evil* (Oxford: Blackwell, 1986), p. 23. See also p. 11.
13. Ibid., p. 67.
14. Ibid., pp. 50, 51.
15. Ibid., p. 52. Surin makes a number of other critical claims concerning theoretical theodicies. He argues that: (i) theoretical theodicies are post-Enlightenment phenomena that postulate a philosophical theism which is not true to traditional Christian views of the Trinity and which tend to ignore the essential social-historical context of traditional theologians in drawing upon ideas from them; (ii) post-Enlightenment and Augustinian theology and epistemology are culturally specific and incommensurable; and (iii) the attempts in theoretical theodicy to apply principles of reason to the problem of evil are futile given the 'fundamentally mysterious' nature of evil and suffering (pp. 52–3).
16. For two recent summaries and overviews of a variety of theologians who criticize theodicy, see Sarah K. Pinnock, *Beyond Theodicy: Jewish and Christian Continental Thinkers Respond to the Holocaust* (Albany, NY: SUNY Press, 2002) and John E. Thiel, *God, Evil and Innocent Suffering: A Theological Reflection* (New York: Crossroad, 2002).
17. On the question of providing sufficient intellectual warrant for religious worldviews in the face of evil, over and against other worldviews, see Michael Scott, 'The Morality of Theodicies', *Religious Studies*, Vol. 32 (1996), 1–13; James Wetzel, 'Can Theodicy be Avoided? The Claim of Unredeemed Evil', *Religious Studies*, Vol. 25 (1989), 1–13, and David O'Connor, 'In Defense of Theoretical Theodicy', *Modern Theology*, Vol. 5 (1988), 61–74.

    James Wetzel makes the point here most succinctly: 'Practical theodicy could not enjoin theology's perpetual silence in the face of evil without beginning to assume the nonbeliever's distance from the resources of faith' (p. 12).
18. Scott, 'The Morality of Theodicies,' 12.
19. Surin, *Theology and the Problem of Evil*, p. 114.
20. Louis Dupré, 'Evil – A Religious Mystery: A Plea For A More Inclusive Model of Theodicy', *Faith and Philosophy*, Vol. 7 (1990), 278.
21. Ibid.
22. The following thoughts with respect to destructive suffering are stimulated and influenced by John Hick, *Evil and the God of Love*, rev. edn (New York:

HarperSanFrancisco, 1977), especially pp. 262–91, 365–86; Ninian Smart, 'Omnipotence, Evil and Superman', *Philosophy*, Vol. 36 (1961); and some of their critics: J. L. Mackie, 'Evil and Omnipotence', *Mind*, Vol. 64 (1955); Antony Flew, 'Divine Omnipotence and Human Freedom' in *New Essays in Philosophical Theology*, ed. Antony Flew and Alistair MacIntyre (London: SCM Press, 1955); Edward H. Madden and Peter H. Hare, *Evil and the Concept of God* (Springfield, IL: Charles C. Thomas, 1968); and G. Stanley Kane, 'The Failure of Soul-Making Theodicy', *International Journal for Philosophy of Religion*, Vol. 6 (1975).
23. Soelle, *Suffering*, p. 125.
24. Michael Washburn, *The Ego and the Dynamic Ground: A Transpersonal Theory of Human Development* (Albany, NY: SUNY Press, 1988), p. 168.
25. Kenneth Surin criticizes the reference in theodicy to further afterlife contexts, insisting that it simply sidesteps the issues (pp. 94–5). However, the harsh reality of destructive suffering *requires* such speculation. This is not to suggest that destructive suffering becomes transformative for the victim (and hence good), but only to hope that healing might occur, however difficult and painful this might be. It merely suggests that opportunities for healing and further spiritual transformation or decline might continue in other life-contexts. Indeed, it seems to me that Christian theism *demands* such a speculative expectation.
26. John Hick and Marilyn McCord Adams raise similar points. Professor Adams writes, 'Many participants in horrors do not recognize or appropriate the positive meanings of their lives ... before they die; many indeed are driven mad by their experiences. Therefore, if such individuals are to have lives that are great goods *to them* on the whole, God must be able to preserve them in life after their death, to place them (à la Hick) in new and nourishing environments where they can profit from Divine instruction on how to integrate their participation in horrors into wholes with positive meanings.' *Horrendous Evils and the Goodness of God*, pp. 83–4. See also especially pp. 167–8, 204–5.

I argue how such afterlife speculation needs initially to stress compassionate healing and to be careful not to deny the absurd nature of the antemortem horror for the victim. The experienced destructive suffering does not contribute to a greater good for the victim. It is not transformative suffering. It is utterly alien to and inhibitive of the transformative dynamic, even if we can understand theologically how and why destructive suffering arises in our world. The hope is not that the victim finds meaning in destructive suffering but only that she or he experiences healing from it within an appropriate afterlife environment. It is the hope that within the Divine intimacy she or he recovers sufficiently, in order to be able to participate creatively again in the dynamic of spiritual growth and transformation.
27. Surin, pp. 104–5.
28. St Thomas writes: 'Augustine says, "There are two evils of the rational creature: one by which it is voluntarily alienated from the supreme good, the other by which it is punished against its will." Punishment and fault are expressly stated by these two. Therefore evil is divided into punishment and fault.' St Thomas Aquinas, *On Evil*, trans. Jean Oesterle (Notre Dame, IN: University of Notre Dame Press, 1995), pt. I, Q. i, art. 4; p. 28.

120 *Notes to pp. 76–80*

Although Thomas is here quoting a spurious attribution to St Augustine, Augustine does maintain this position. See *De Natura Boni of Saint Augustine: A Translation with an Introduction and Commentary*, trans. and ed. A. Anthony Moon (Washington, DC: The Catholic University of America Press, 1955), especially pp. 9, 34–41, 70–1. As Michael Latzer points out, for Augustine and Thomas 'the only authentic instances of evil are sin and the punishment of sin, that is, the evils which derive from the wrongdoing of rational creatures' (p. 62). 'The Nature of Evil: Leibniz and his Medieval Background', *The Modern Schoolman*, Vol. 71 (1993), 59–69.

29. Morton T. Kelsey, *Healing and Christianity: In Ancient Thought and Modern Times* (New York: Harper & Row, 1973), pp. 20, 21. For details of the Service for the Sick, see especially pp. 15–22.

 Kelsey speculates on the possible historical developments in the church that lead to the view that all sickness is to be attributed to sin or the punishment for sin (pp. 200–38). This trend is highlighted in the twelfth century in the formal transformation of the order for visiting and anointing of the sick into the sacrament of *Unctio Extrema* – administered primarily or only at the time of death – and solely, in the words of St Thomas Aquinas, as 'a spiritual remedy, since it avails for the remission of sins...' (p. 209). It is very curious how in Christian scholastic theology *all* suffering comes to be connected with sin, especially given the explicit admonitions of Jesus in the New Testament that not all suffering is a result of sin (for example, in *Luke* 13:2–5 and *John* 9:1–3). Related to this, a rich patristic theology of healing, grounded in the New Testament emphasis on the practice, is almost wholly ignored in later medieval theology. In the Roman Catholic Church, in the 1960s, the Constitution on the Sacred Liturgy of the Second Vatican Council provided significant stimulus in the renewal of a theology of the sick. The document insists that the sacrament is not only for those who are near-death, it explicitly names the sacrament as 'more fittingly' the 'anointing of the sick', and it explicitly distinguishes it from last communion (Viaticum) (pp. 241–2).

30. See, for example, John R. Sachs, 'Resurrection or Reincarnation? The Christian Doctrine of Purgatory', *Reincarnation or Resurrection?*, *Concilium*, Vol. 5 (1993), 81–7, for a brief overview of the doctrine, including traditional official definitions and some contemporary interpretations.

31. These afterlife possibilities of purgatory and rebirth are the subject of Chapter 5, where the focus is on continual spiritual transformation in these afterlife contexts. However, I would like to stress here especially the importance in contemporary conceptions of reincarnation and purgatory to articulate a process of healing from destructive suffering.

32. Baron F. von Hügel, 'What Do We Mean By Heaven? And What Do We Mean By Hell?' in *Essays and Addresses on the Philosophy of Religion*, Vol. I (London: J. M. Dent, 1921), p. 203.

5 Afterlife Beliefs

1. I have chosen here, along with Marcus Borg, to translate the Greek '*oiktirmon*' as 'compassion'. Stephen Hawkes-Teeples informed me that this word

is not the common Greek word for 'mercy' in the New Testament, being found only once in *Luke* and once in *The Letter of James*. Borg thinks that it was part of the *Gospel of Q*, the verse being present in a redacted form ('perfect') in *Matthew* 5: 48.

Also, Borg writes: 'Quite often the Hebrew words for *compassion* and *compassionate* are translated into English as *mercy* and *merciful*. But compassion is quite different from mercy, and being compassionate quite different from being merciful. In English *mercy* and *merciful* most commonly imply a superior in relationship to a subordinate, and also a situation of wrongdoing: one is merciful towards somebody to whom one has the right (or power) to act otherwise. *Compassion* suggests something else. To paraphrase William Blake, mercy wears a human face, and compassion a human heart.' Marcus Borg, *Meeting Jesus Again for the First Time: The Historical Jesus and the Heart of Contemporary Faith* (New York: HarperSanFrancisco, 1994), pp. 46–8, 62 note 1.

Perhaps the traditional stress in Christian theodicy on retributive punishment has influenced somewhat this tendency in translation. Borg also notes how in Hebrew the singular form of compassion means 'womb'. In reference to God, then, compassion carries with it powerful images of maternal carrying, birthing, holding, nourishing and protecting (pp. 48–9).
2. Dorothee Soelle, *Suffering*, trans. Everett R. Kalin (Philadelphia: Fortress Press, 1975), p. 114.
3. For a fascinating historical survey of this speculation see Alan E. Bernstein, *The Formation of Hell: Death and Retribution in the Ancient and Early Christian Worlds* (Ithaca, NY: Cornell University Press, 1993). For a fine philosophical systematization and exploration of the various views of hell, see Jonathan L. Kvanvig, *The Problem of Hell* (New York: Oxford University Press, 1993).
4. Alice K. Turner, *The History of Hell* (New York: Harcourt Brace, 1993), p. 3. From a recent Gallup poll.
5. Fyodor Dostoyevsky, *The Brothers Karamazov*, trans. Constance Garnett (New York: The Modern Library, 1929), p. 25.
6. Augustine, *Concerning The City of God against the Pagans*, ed. Henry Bettenson (New York: Penguin Books, 1980), XXI. 2–9; p. 985.
7. John Hick, *Death and Eternal Life* (Glasgow: William Collins, 1979), pp. 200–01.
8. Other significant proponents of the doctrine of universal salvation include John Scotus Erigena, Giordano Bruno, Spinoza, and Schleiermacher. See Baron F. von Hügel, 'What Do We Mean By Heaven? And What Do We Mean By Hell?' in *Essays and Addresses on the Philosophy of Religion*, Vol. I (London: J. M. Dent, 1921), p. 220. Also, for a historical outline of the belief and a survey of current Roman Catholic responses to the issue, focusing especially on Hans Urs von Balthasar, see John R. Sachs, 'Current Eschatology: Universal Salvation and the Problem of Evil,' *Theological Studies*, Vol. 52 (1991), 227–54.
9. Augustine, *The City of God*, XXI.17; p. 995. My emphases.
10. Ibid., XXI.18; p. 998.
11. The other themes of theodicy in Augustine's writings are the privation of the good, the aesthetic, and the teleological. With regard to the teleological and the aesthetic, he writes: 'When happiness is the lot of those who sin

not, the world is perfect; and it is no less perfect when unhappiness is the lot of sinners. But because those souls are not lacking which become unhappy when they sin and happy when they do right, the world is always full and perfect with all natures. For sin and the punishment of sin are not properly natures, but conditions of nature: the former being voluntary, the latter is applied in expiation, so that nature is ordered where it may not be a disgrace, and made to conform to the glory of the universe, so that the penalty of sin corrects the disgrace of sin.' Augustine, *St Augustine on Free Will*, trans. Carroll Mason Sparrow (Charlottesville: University of Virginia, 1947), III, ix, 26; p. 108.

For an even more intricate aesthetic balancing within which hell finds its natural place, see a critical account of the view of St Anselm by Frank Burch Brown: 'The Beauty of Hell: Anselm on God's Eternal Design', *Journal of Religion*, Vol. 73 (1993), 329–56. Professor Brown also proposes an interpretation of hell which corresponds in some respects to the view I am illustrating here.

12. Augustine, *The City of God*, XXI.23, p. 1002.
13. The importance of this contrast between heaven and hell applies even for contemporary Roman Catholic theologians who distinguish the logical status of afterlife possibilities in terms of fact (salvation) and possibility (hell). See Peter Phan, 'Contemporary Context and Issues in Eschatology', *Theological Studies*, Vol. 55 (1994) 516, 531. In that essay Phan gives a critical overview of the document *De quibusdam quaestionibus actualibus circa eschatologiam* (1992) by the International Theological Commission. This document is translated as 'Some Current Questions in Eschatology,' *Irish Theological Quarterly*, Vol. 58 (1992), 209–43.
14. Hugh of St Victor, *On The Sacraments of the Christian Faith*, II.xviii.2, as quoted in John Hick, *Evil and the God of Love*, rev. edn (New York: HarperSanFrancisco, 1977), p. 92.
15. Augustine, *The City of God*, XXII.30, p. 1090.
16. As quoted in Gene Outka, *Agape: An Ethical Analysis* (New Haven: Yale University Press, 1972), p. 160. From Donald D. Evans, *The Logic of Self Involvement* (New York: Herder & Herder, 1969), p. 134.
17. Peter Phan, 'Contemporary Context,' 531–2. Both Karl Rahner and Hans Urs von Balthasar stress in their theology this point of hope for universal salvation. See especially von Balthasar, *Dare We Hope That All Men Be Saved?* (San Francisco: Ignatius Press, 1988).
18. Donald D. Evans, *Spirituality and Human Nature* (Albany, NY: SUNY Press, 1993), p. 90. Narcissism is a major theme of this book. See especially Section 1.II.
19. Karl Rahner writes: mysticism has 'a paradigmatic character, an exemplary function, to make clear to the Christian what really happens and is meant when his faith tells him that God's self-communication is given to him in grace and accepted in freedom whenever he believes, hopes and loves.' Karl Rahner, *The Practice of Faith: A Handbook of Contemporary Spirituality*, ed. Karl Lehmann and Albert Raffelt (New York: Crossroad, 1984), p. 70.
20. Karl F. Morrison, *'I am You': The Hermeneutics of Empathy in Western Literature, Theology, and Art* (Princeton: Princeton University Press, 1988), pp. 17–18.

21. Ibid., p. 17.
22. Von Hügel insists on a transformation which is a supernatural continuance and extension of a consciousness realized in *this* life-time. He writes that heaven is not to be understood 'as the supreme rule and reward of average earthly honesty, decency, and justice' but 'as the deepest meaning and the final assaugement [sic] of the soul's thirst for more and other than these things.' 'What Do We Mean By Heaven?', 200, 199.
23. Dostoyevsky, *The Brothers Karamazov*, pp. 400–1.
24. Von Hügel, 'What Do We Mean By Heaven?', pp. 216–17. He also says: 'The lost spirits will persist, according to the degree of their permanent defection, in their claimfulness and envious self-isolation, in their niggardly pain at the sight or thought of the unmatchable greatness and goodness of other souls.' 'The lost souls are left to the pain of stainedness and self-contraction; they do not attain to, since they do not really will, the suffering of purification and expansive harmonisation.' pp. 217, 219.
25. Donald Evans writes: 'Gabriel Marcel, for example, sees what I call *radical evil* as an "egocentricity" which arises from a lack of participation in being, an inner emptiness.' *Spirituality and Human Nature*, p. 208.
26. Irenaeus writes: 'And to as many as continue in their love towards God, does He grant communion with Him. But communion with God is life and light, and the enjoyment of all the benefits which He has in store. But on as many as, according to their own choice, depart from God, He inflicts that separation from Himself which they have chosen of their own accord ... God, however, does not punish them immediately of Himself, but that punishment falls upon them because they are destitute of all that is good. ... It is in this matter just as occurs in the case of a flood of light: those who have blinded themselves, or have been blinded by others, are forever deprived of the enjoyment of light. It is not, [however], that the light has inflicted upon them the penalty of blindness, but it is that the blindness itself has brought calamity upon them.' *Irenaeus Against Heresies*, *The Ante-Nicene Fathers*, I, ed. Alexander Roberts and James Donaldson (Grand Rapids, Michigan: Wm. B. Eerdmans, 1979), V, 27, 2. My thanks to Bill Loewe, for bringing this reference to my attention.

   This portrayal of hell as the lack of the fulfilment of spiritual potential and the absence of beatific communion is also present in Augustine's writings, but notice how he frames the question in terms of anger and fear, and does not mention *agape*: 'If one were to experience [the anger of God], even the slightest aspect of it that can be imagined, taken by itself: to perish from the kingdom of God, to be an exile from the City of God, to be alienated from the life of God, to lack the immensity of God's sweetness, which he reserved for those who fear him and perfected for those hoping in him, that fate, if it were eternal, would nonetheless be so great a punishment that no torment which we know here, were it to last for as many ages as we can conceive, may be compared with it.' (*Enchiridion* 29.112.65–71). As quoted in Alan E. Bernstein, *The Formation of Hell*, pp. 330–1.
27. C. S. Lewis (ed.), *George MacDonald: An Anthology* (New York: Macmillan, 1948), p. 85. See also Keith E. Yandell, 'The Doctrine of Hell and Moral Philosophy', *Religious Studies*, Vol. 28 (1992), especially 79–80, 81, 85, and George Grant, *Philosophy in the Mass Age* (Toronto: University of Toronto

124   *Notes to pp. 91–6*

Press, 1995), p. 36. For a contemporary Roman Catholic version of this view of hell, see Dermot A. Lane, *Keeping Hope Alive: Stirrings in Christian Theology* (Mahwah, NJ: Paulist Press, 1996), pp. 140–2. Regarding the views of Plotinus and the Pseudo-Dionysius, see Michael Stoeber, *Evil and the Mystics' God* (London: Macmillan Press, 1992), pp. 22–30.

28. Jean Vanier, *Becoming Human* (Toronto: House of Anansi Press, 1998), pp. 9–10.
29. Simone Weil, 'The Love of God and Affliction', *Simone Weil: Writings Selected With an Introduction*, ed. Eric O. Springsted (Mayknoll, NY: Orbis Books, 1998), p. 44.
30. Marilyn McCord Adams, 'The Problem of Hell: A Problem of Evil for Christians', in *Reasoned Faith: Essays in Philosophical Theology in Honour of Norman Kretzmann*, ed. Eleanore Stump (Ithaca, NY: Cornell University Press, 1993), p. 313.
31. Dostoyevsky, *The Brothers Karamazov*, p. 320.
32. Karl Rahner suggests a similar argument in his brief and highly speculative discussion on purgatory: 'If there is such a state as purgatory which does not come into existence merely by an external decree and intervention of God, but is a connatural consequence of the nature of the plural human being, then I could imagine that it might offer opportunities and scope for a postmortal history of freedom to someone who had been denied such a history in his earthly life.' (p. 191) 'Purgatory', *Faith and Ministry*, in *Theological Investigations*, Vol. 19, trans. Edward Quinn (New York: Crossroads, 1983), pp. 181–93.
33. Von Hügel, 'What Do We Mean By Heaven?,' p. 203.
34. Sayers summarizes this traditional view of purgatory: 'What is left to be done in Purgatory is the purging of the *reatus*, so far as there may not have been time or opportunity to do this on earth, and, especially, the cleansing of the soul from the *stain of sin*. By this is meant the damage done to the soul by the habit of sinfulness – the coarsening of fibre, and the clouding of the mind and imagination ... So long as there remains in the soul the least trace of consent to sin, this clouding and coarsening remain to fetter the will and judgement. Only when the clear sight and tender conscience are restored is the soul set free to stand before the unveiled light of the presence of God, which otherwise it could not endure.' (p. 58) For an illuminating outline of the traditional Catholic view of purgatory, with special attention to the developments in St Thomas Aquinas and Dante, see the 'Introduction' by Dorothy L. Sayers to *The Comedy of Dante Alighieri The Florentine, Cantica II: Purgatory* (Middlesex, England: Penguin Books, 1955), especially pp. 54–61.
35. Paul Tillich makes a similar point in his reflection on purgatory: 'Purgatory is a state in which the soul is "purged" from the distorting elements of temporal existence. In Catholic doctrine, mere suffering does the purging. Besides the psychological impossibility of imagining uninterrupted periods of mere suffering, it is a theological mistake to derive transformation from pain alone instead of from grace which gives blessedness without pain.' *Systematic Theology*, Vol. 3 (Chicago: University of Chicago Press, 1963), p. 417.
36. John R. Sachs writes: 'In the East, purgation after death was seen as a necessary process of education and maturation preparing the soul for the vision

of God. In the West, more emphasis was placed on the issues of justice and retribution, so that purgatory was viewed more in a penal context' (p. 82). For a brief overview of the doctrine, including traditional official definitions and some contemporary interpretations, see 'Resurrection or Reincarnation? The Christian Doctrine of Purgatory,' in *Reincarnation or Resurrection?, Concilium*, ed. Herman Häring and Johann-Baptist Metz (London: SCM Press 1993), pp. 81–7.

37. Dermot Lane, *Keeping Hope Alive* (New York: Paulist Press, 1996), pp. 147–8. Also in regards to the idea of spiritual transformation, Peter Phan calls for some expansion on the Roman Catholic version of purgatory that is espoused in *De quibusdam quaestionibus actualibus circa eschatologiam* by the International Theological Commission in 1992. He writes: 'It lacks an anthropology to account for the necessity of "purification". Its language is still impersonal and objectivistic. It speaks of "stains" resulting from sins that need to be removed. Missing is an understanding of the human person as a multileveled being whose innermost center requires a process of integration and transformation to be fully united with God, even though guilt has been forgiven.' Peter Phan, 'Contemporary Context and Issues in Eschatology', p. 519.

Both Phan and Lane are following in part the lead of Karl Rahner who writes that 'because of the many levels of man, and consequently because of the unequal phases in the process of becoming in which he reaches fulfilment in all of his dimensions, it [the Catholic doctrine of purgatory] seems to teach that there is a process of maturation "after" death for the whole person. It is a process in which his basic decision permeates the whole length and breadth of his reality.' *Foundations of Christian Faith: An Introduction to the Idea of Christianity*, trans. William V. Dych (New York, Seabury Press, 1978), pp. 441–2. To the concerns expressed by Phan and Lane, I would add the importance of the process of *healing* in contemporary conceptions of purgatory.

For conjecture concerning the possibility of purgatory as a realm suitable for further transformation to the divine life, see Origen (185–254 AD), *On First Principles*, especially Book 4, Chapter 3, where he gives a fascinating speculative account in terms of detailed allegorical interpretation of scripture. He writes 'just as the souls born on this earth of ours either come back from the lower world to higher places by their desire of better things and so take a human body or descend as far to us from better places, so also those places that are above in the firmament are inhabited by some souls that have progressed from our abode to better things, and also by other souls that have fallen from heavenly places as far as to the firmament but have not sinned so greatly as to be thrust down to the lower places that we inhabit ... The firmament is a lower world by comparison with the higher heaven, and this earth that we inhabit is called a lower world by comparison with the firmament, and further, by comparison with the lower world that is under us, we are said to be heaven, so that what to some is the lower world is to others heaven.' *On First Principles*, Book 4, Chapter 3, Section 10, from Origen, *The Classics of Western Spirituality*, trans. Rowan A. Greer (New York: Paulist Press, 1979), p. 198.

Geddes MacGregor gives an interesting discussion of the controversies surrounding Origen in a chapter in *Reincarnation in Christianity: A New Vision of the Role of Rebirth in Christian Thought* (Wheaton, IL: Quest, 1978), pp. 48–62. It is also interesting to note Joseph Wilson Trigg's evaluation of the effectiveness of Origen's theology as theodicy: Origen's theology 'is a vision of extraordinary moral grandeur and perhaps as satisfactory a solution, from the perspective of faith, to the problem of theodicy as has ever been suggested'. *Origen: The Bible and Philosophy in the Third-century Church* (Atlanta: John Knox Press, 1983), p. 111.

No doubt such a claim is considerably circumscribed by the fact that the Church eventually rejects Origen's views concerning the nature of the resurrected body, universal salvation, and the pre-existence of souls, and that his Christology and methodologies come under criticism. Still, Origen's influence on Christian theological developments is momentous (for example, in terms of the establishment of the scriptural canon, the methods of biblical exegesis, and the theology of spiritual ascent) and it is significant, as Trigg notes, that '[the] twentieth century has witnessed an extraordinary rebirth of interest in and appreciation of Origen among Catholic theologians, including Karl Rahner, Hans Urs von Balthasar, Jean Cardinal Daniélou, and Henri Cardinal de Lubac' (pp. 256–7).

Finally, I should also note the view of Keith Ward, who, though he does not speak of the condition as 'purgatory', suggests that: 'It might be better to think of there being a continuum from the deepest Hell to the most blissful Paradise, with many worlds between, between which souls can progress in greater knowledge of their true nature and relation to God, still enduring conflict and frustration to varying degrees ... They enter the dream-worlds of death, a whole continuum of worlds, from worlds of apparently endless suffering to worlds of apparently timeless bliss. They enter the world which best expresses their spiritual state at death, and they then progress through these worlds, or remain in them, in accordance with their own continuing spiritual development.' *Religion and Human Nature* (Oxford: Clarendon Press, 1998) 275–6. The contemporary development of this theme originates in John Hick, *Death and Eternal Life* (Glasgow: William Collins, 1976).

38. Paul Tillich briefly explores and criticizes the possibilities of traditional views of purgatory, reincarnation, and the Protestant 'doctrine of the intermediary state between death and resurrection.' He argues that the first is deficient in its exclusive emphasis on suffering and punishment, the second contains problems in securing personal identity connections over various embodiments, and the third has issues surrounding the envisioned disembodied condition. He himself seems to defend a qualified version of purgatory, one where the idea of a transformative dynamic of process can be included in the afterlife vision: 'eternity is neither timeless identity nor permanent change, as the latter occurs in the temporal process. Time and change are present in the depth of Eternal Life, but they are contained within the eternal unity of the Divine Life. If we combine this solution with the idea that no individual destiny is separated from the destiny of the universe, we have the framework within which the great question of the development of the individual in Eternal Life can at least find a limited

theological answer.' *Systematic Theology*, Vol. 3, quotes are from pp. 417, 418; see 415–19.

39. See, for example, G. C. Nayak, *Evil, Karma and Reincarnation* (Santiniketan, West Bengal: Centre of Advanced Study in Philosophy, Visva-Bharati, 1973). Nayak argues that retributive rebirth provides the most effective theodicy.

40. For example, the *Laws of Manu*, an important book on Hindu *dharma* (duty, law) states, 'Thus, in consequence of a remnant of the guilt are born idiots, dumb, blind, deaf and deformed men, *despised by the virtuous.*' As quoted in Klaus K. Klostermaier, *A Survey of Hinduism*, 2nd edn (Albany, NY: SUNY Press, 1994), p. 178. My emphasis.

41. Rebirth is a belief common to the Kabbalah since at least the late twelfth century. Gershom Scholem provides a brief historical overview of the belief (what he calls *gilgul* – transmigration) in *Kabbalah* (New York: Meridian Books, 1978), pp. 344–8. Scholem writes: '*gilgul* provides an opportunity for restitution. While some emphasized more strongly the aspect of justice in transmigration, and some that of mercy, its singular purpose was always the purification of the soul and the opportunity, in a new trial, to improve its deeds.' (p. 346)

For a modern Hindu perspective of soul-making rebirth, see Sri Aurobindo Ghose, *The Problem of Rebirth*, in *Sri Aurobindo Birth Centenary Library*, Vol. 16 (Pondicherry, India: Sri Aurobindo Ashram Trust, 1971). For modern Christian proposals, see: Anonymous, *Meditations on the Tarot: A Journey into Christian Hermeticism*, trans. Robert A. Powell (Warwick, NY: Amity House, 1985), especially pp. 92–4, 360–2; and books by Geddes MacGregor, *Reincarnation in Christianity: A New Vision of the Role of Rebirth in Christian Thought* (Wheaton, Illinois: Quest, 1978), and *Reincarnation as a Christian Hope* (Totowa, New Jersey: Barnes & Noble, 1982). Andrew Chignell draws on the theme of reincarnation in responding to the problem of infant suffering. See 'The Problem of Infant Suffering,' *Religious Studies*, Vol. 34 (1998) 205–17 and 'Infant Suffering Revisited,' *Religious Studies*, Vol. 37 (2001) 475–84. Also, for an interesting discussion of some of the conditions and issues surrounding the growing appeal of rebirth in the west, see David S. Toolan, 'Reincarnation and Modern Gnosis', *Reincarnation or Resurrection?*, *Concilium*, ed. Herman Häring and Johann-Baptist Metz (London: SCM Press, 1993), pp. 32–45.

Both rebirth and purgatory are explored in a preliminary way in Michael Stoeber, *Evil and the Mystics' God*, Chapter 10, and in 'Personal Identity and Rebirth,' *Religious Studies*, Vol. 26 (1990) 493–500. In those writings I suggested that certain versions of soul-making rebirth are more plausible and cogent than those of probationary or soul-making purgatory. My view has since changed in support of purgatory, in light especially of considerations on the nature and effects of destructive suffering. Even if soul-making rebirth is true, one can still imagine an intermediary realm were certain healing and learning might occur that cannot happen in this world. I think the possibility of soul-making purgatory does not necessarily discredit the appropriateness of this world as a soul-making environment, as I previously thought. Moreover, aside from some of the evidence surrounding paradeath phenomena that supports the possibility, there is great mystery surround-

ing birth and death which is perhaps also suggestive of the possibility of an intermediary realm or realms of existence.
42. Sri Aurobindo Ghose, *The Problem of Rebirth*; Keith Ward, *Religion and Human Nature*, p. 53.
43. An anonymous reader at Palgrave Macmillan kindly pointed out the major significance of the Bodhisattva ideal in regard to this idea of soul-making rebirth.
44 The effectiveness of retributive rebirth as a theme of theodicy has been brought into question by various writers, including: Paul Edwards 'The Case Against Reincarnation,' *Free Inquiry*, Vol. 6, No. 4 (1986), pp. 24–43 and Vol. 7, Nos 1–3 (1987), pp. 38–48, 38–49, 46–53, and *Reincarnation: A Critical Examination* (New York: Prometheus Books, 1996); and Whitley R. P. Kaufman, 'Karma, Rebirth, and the Problem of Evil,' *Philosophy East & West*, Vol. 55 (2005), 15–32. Kaufman questions the effectiveness of rebirth in explaining 'the presence in the world of human suffering and misery' (19), even if it were true, given problems associated with the lack of past-life memories, the apparent disproportion of suffering for specific misdeeds, the question of the infinite regress of past karma, the problem of explaining death as evil, the problem of free will with respect to karma, and the fact that the theory is not publicly verifiable.

The underlying issue which seriously hinders the effectiveness of Kaufman's critique (and the concerns of Edwards as well) is that he fails to distinguish between retributive and soul-making versions of rebirth. Effective afterlife visions need to presume that all punishment (even apparently retributive) serves some reformative purpose. In such views of reformative rebirth not all suffering – and certainly not destructive suffering – is considered a retributive consequence of one's specific misdeeds. Effective soul-making rebirth moves away from hardline and strict mechanistic pictures of *karma*, suggesting how devastating tragedy sometimes simply befalls a person, regardless of his or her previous attitudes and behaviour. It introduces elements of chance into the picture and insists that all just punishment needs to contain reformative elements. Indeed, such views of soul-making rebirth themselves do not really even attempt to 'explain the presence in the world of human suffering and misery' (19), though they fit within a framework of effective theodicy. Like probationary purgatory, they function rather as a compassionate vehicle or medium of human progression or regression, one that secures that the victims of incredible misfortune will be given opportunities to recover and continue their spiritual journeys in other life-contexts. This might include also elements of reform, for which past-life memories are not required in order for it to obtain. These qualifications of rebirth take the bite out of those criticisms of Kaufman that are most serious: the lack of past-life memories, the apparent disproportion of suffering for specific misdeeds, and the question of the infinite regress of past karma. See also the relevant discussions of purgatory and rebirth in endnote 47.
45. Karl Rahner raises the possibility of initiating dialogue between eastern traditions and Christianity on the question of rebirth through reflection on the possible nature of purgatory: 'Let me just call attention to the question whether in the Catholic notion of an "interval", which seems so obsolete at

first, there could not be a starting point for coming to terms in a better and more positive way with the doctrine of the "transmutation of souls" or of "reincarnation", which is so widespread in eastern cultures and is regarded there as something to be taken for granted. This is a possibility, at least on the presupposition that this reincarnation is not understood as a fate for man which will never end and will continue on forever in time.' *Foundations of Christian Faith: An Introduction to the Idea of Christianity*, trans. William V. Dych (New York: Seabury Press, 1978), p. 442.

Ovey Mohammed also explores briefly this possibility of relating soul-making rebirth to purgatory, suggesting that there are parallels when these views are conceived in terms of the dynamics of spiritual transformation: 'Rebirth affirms that God's love is so infinite that God gives us the opportunity to grow until we achieve perfection. If some Christians believe that nothing defiled shall see God and recognize that most of us need further purification at death, and if it is this recognition that has prompted the doctrine of purgatory, then the doctrine of rebirth as an opportunity for further purification, for working off our bad *karma*, has its parallel in the doctrine of purgatory. Through the doctrine of purgatory, it is possible for Christians to hope that, because God's nature is one of love, no one finally fails to make the journey to God. From a universalist perspective, then, the law of *karma* and rebirth can be harmonized with the doctrine of purgatory without denying the possibility of hell (p. 670).' 'Jesus and Krishna', *Journal of Ecumenical Studies*, Vol. 26 (1989), 664–80.

However, the degree to which rebirth is possibly compatible with other central aspects of Christian doctrine is a complicated question. It seems clear to me that a traditional, strictly retributive view of rebirth is incompatible with essential Christian teachings. But contemporary views of soul-making rebirth seem to overcome some of the major theological problems raised for rebirth by Christian theologians, who tend to focus in their criticisms on versions of retributive rebirth or to understand it only in association with traditional Hindu or Buddhist views of spiritual liberation that differ radically from Christian conceptions of salvation.

Although retributive rebirth in the traditional Hindu context tends to be associated with a cyclical view of creation which postulates a non-created soul and an individualistic, spiritual ideal of disembodied liberation from this world, contemporary views of rebirth as a vehicle of spiritual transformation seem possibly congruous with many Christian theological perspectives. For example, it seems compatible with Christian views of God, of a first creation of the soul, and of sin and grace. Also it can be drawn into various Christological perspectives, and related to Christian eschatological ideas of time, community, and history.

In *Keeping Hope Alive*, Dermot A. Lane focuses on these themes in a brief criticism of retributive rebirth (pp. 167–73). However, rebirth considered as a medium of spiritual transformation seems possibly congenial with the following major Christian theological threads: a linear view of time which is conceived in terms of eschatological purposes that are grounded and embraced by eternity; a view of a God 'who creates and sustains everything in existence' and towards which humanity is oriented in the 'hope for a personally transforming full communion'; and an anthropological orientation that involves a this-worldly 'social and political responsibility for the world', one which acknowledges the relevance of human history and the aspiration 'to gather up the whole of human, historical and cosmic life into a New Creation' (pp. 172–3). That is to say, soul-making rebirth seems compatible with an eschatological vision that supposes a historical people journeying in grace towards an embodied communion of *all* of humanity in loving intimacy with God and each other, where the final resurrection involves the spiritual transformation and divinization of embodied beings in union with God. This outline corresponds roughly with the anonymous Christian Hermeticist's perspective given in *Meditations on the Tarot*.

One significant point seems perhaps incongruous with traditional Christian views. The Catholic resurrection ideal proposes the singularity and uniqueness of each individual, while in rebirth the bodies of each soul-individuation would seem to be transcended by each particular new incarnation. 'Soul' in some views of rebirth means the essence of the person, the most fundamental characteristics of who one is. The general idea is that this essence is the transmigrating phenomena. In an incarnate person the body comes to be the expression of this essence through the soul-body integration, and the medium by which it interacts with other people and the created world. Although some views of rebirth might suppose the uniqueness and dignity of each embodied soul as well as a full ongoing body–mind integration within one's condition of material embodiment, a sharply dualistic anthropology seems to be a necessary feature of this version of rebirth, a view which would appear to call into question traditional claims of the individuation of the soul according only to a single body.

I am currently working on an essay that explores the possible nature and dynamics of a soul in rebirth, drawing especially on the thought of the anonymous Christian Hermeticist in *Meditations on the Tarot*. I expect that the Christian anthropology of Edith Stein will also helpful in clarifying an intelligible and plausible soul–body integration that might occur in rebirth. The view seems consistent with Christian views of the sacredness and significance of each individual life-embodiment. Life, understood as the transformative movement towards divinized communion, can be thought to sustain an imperative to draw constantly on all of one's shared resources in the hope-filled journey towards the spiritual ideal. Christian resurrection ideals typically suggest the spiritual transformation of that same, singular body. Rebirth postulates a whole series of soul embodiments or individuations, so even in contemporary versions of rebirth which postulate an embodied ideal that involves a transfigured body, the resurrection body could not be a transformation of a singular earthly soul–body individuation. They must somehow integrate factors of multi-embodiments in its resurrection ideal. It would have to be made clear how the resurrection ideal might be related to the transfiguring features of every incarnated body. This issue also points towards related philosophical problems pertaining to personal identity continuity between embodiments, which I am also exploring in that essay.

Clearly there are difficulties in framing rebirth in terms of traditional Christian anthropology. Also, like the doctrine of purgatory, there is the question of the lack of explicit scriptural references to the belief (though various sources have cited passages as possibly supportive: *Job* 33: 29; *Psalms* 105: 8; *Ecclesiastes* 1: 4, 12: 7; *Isaiah* 43: 5–7; *Matthew* 16: 13–15, 17: 9–13; *Mark* 8: 27–30; *Luke* 9: 7–9, 9: 18–21; *John* 1: 21). Nevertheless, it seems to me that some contemporary versions of soul-making rebirth could be more compatible with many central Christian teachings than some theologians might assume.

See also a discussion of issues associated with this question of rebirth and Christianity in John J. Heaney, *The Sacred and the Psychic: Parapsychology and Christian Theology* (New York: Paulist Press, 1984), pp. 211–20, and in John Hick, *Death and Eternal Life*, especially pp. 363–96.

46. Near-death and pre-death experiences point to the possibility of a continued consciousness in other planes of existence. This evidence supports the possibility of purgatory, but it is controversial and highly ambiguous. For good overviews of the phenomena, as well as a helpful bibliographies, see: Heather Botting, 'Medico-Scientific Assumptions Regarding Paradeath Phenomena: Explanation or Obfuscation?', *Critical Reflections on the Paranormal*, ed. Michael Stoeber and Hugo Meynell (Albany, NY: SUNY Press, 1996), pp. 159–76; and Carol Zaleski, *Otherworldy Journeys: Accounts of Near-Death Experience in Medieval and Modern Times* (New York: Oxford University Press, 1987) and *The Life of the World to Come: Near-Death Experience and Christian Hope* (New York: Oxford University Press, 1996).

In the case of rebirth the evidence is controversial and ambiguous as well, though it seems stronger. The evidence can, I think, be interpreted in such a way to support positively one's belief in it. It is largely anecdotal, spontaneous, and unsubstantiated. But recent scientific research and formal investigation by Ian Stevenson, a professor of psychiatry and neurology at the University of Virginia, has provided much more credible evidence. He has collected since the early 1970s information concerning children, mainly but not exclusively from South Asia, who narrate imaged memories of past life happenings, and/or evince unusual behavioural patterns that correspond to previous personalities, and/or possess physical traces in the form of birthmarks or other disfigurements that correspond to injuries of the postulated previous personality. For an overview of his research, see Ian Stevenson, *Children Who Remember Previous Lives: A Question of Reincarnation* (Charlottesville: University Press of Virginia, 1987).

Stevenson and his colleagues attempt to confirm or deny the memories of the children by investigating the lives of recently deceased candidates. In a significant number of cases, the correspondences have proven remarkable, where the child's detailed knowledge about people, places, and/or events is confirmed, and/or where their behaviour and/or physical disfigurement corresponds remarkably with that of a deceased candidate. There is agreement even among some sceptics of rebirth that the phenomenon is significant enough to demand a reasonable explanation, though there is much controversy regarding claims in support of rebirth.

I mentioned in the last endnote that I am currently working on an essay that explores the possible nature and dynamics of a soul in rebirth. In that essay I will also explore in more detail the debate concerning the merits of Stevenson's work. Even if the evidence remains inconclusive, it appears that

Stevenson's research provides some non-subjective, corroborated evidence in support of afterlife claims that reasonable people might deem credible but not conclusive. Moreover, if some past-life memories are accessible, this ensures personal identity connections of a particular soul through various human incarnations. In my essay I plan to develop this line of argument in more detail and explore also the issues and possible conditions surrounding multiple soul-embodiments.

At this point in time I can close this discussion with the following observations. Even if the various questions facing these postulations of rebirth and purgatory are answered satisfactorily, one cannot presently know with certainty if these afterlife possibilities are true. I doubt that the narrative of spiritual life that I put forward in this book requires one even to maintain these afterlife beliefs in order for it to unfold positively. Still, these afterlife views are intelligible and coherent, and they neatly reflect commonsense approaches to learning, personal development, and moral and spiritual growth. Most importantly, in terms of this book, they are postulations of hope for those suffering severe affliction, hope that there might be some future afterlife healing from their pain and further opportunities of spiritual growth and transformation. Despite his own scepticism towards rebirth, Keith Ward acknowledges the significance of the theory as a postulate of hope in the face of extremely destructive suffering: 'the idea of rebirth does enshrine a hope for the possibility of spiritual progress and development, even for those whose earthly lives seem to make such a hope impossible. That is a hope that must be basic for any religion of devotion to a truly gracious and loving God, and there must be some way of providing for it in any religion of grace. Even if the hypothesis of rebirth is rejected, that hope is one of the things that Gaudiya Vaishnavism has to teach the Christian tradition.' *Religion and Human Nature*, p. 75.
47. In correspondence.
48. Soelle, *Suffering*, p. 22.
49. Ibid. See also Cynthia Crysdale, *Embracing Travail: Retrieving the Cross Today* (New York: Continuum, 1999). Her book sensitively explores various avenues of Christian redemption, with special attention to the perspective of the victims of sin.
50. Soelle, *Suffering*, p. 100.

Bibliography

Abhishiktānanda, *Ascent to the Depth of the Heart: The Spiritual Diary (1948–1973) of Swāmī Abhishiktānanda (Dom H. Le Saux)*, A selection, edited with introduction and notes, by Raimon Panikkar, David Fleming and James Stuart (trs) (Delhi: ISPCK, 1998).

Adams, Marilyn McCord, *Horrendous Evils and the Goodness of God* (Ithaca, NY: Cornell University Press, 1999).

———, 'The Problem of Hell: A Problem of Evil for Christians', in *Reasoned Faith*, ed. Eleanore Stump (Ithaca, NY: Cornell University Press, 1993), pp. 301–27.

———, 'Redemptive Suffering: A Christian Solution to the Problem of Evil', *Rationality, Religious Belief, and Moral Commitment: New Essays in the Philosophy of Religion*, ed. Robert Audi and William Wainwright (Ithaca, NY: Cornell University Press, 1986), pp. 248–67.

Aïvanhov, Omraam Mikhaël, *Life Force*, Vol. 5 of *Complete Works* (Fréjus, France: Prosveta, 1993).

Allen, Diogenes, 'Natural Evil and the Love of God', *Religious Studies*, Vol. 16 (1980), 439–56.

Anonymous, *Meditations on the Tarot: A Journey into Christian Hermeticism*, trans. Robert A. Powell (Rockport, MA: Element, 1985).

Augustine, St, *St Augustine on Free Will*, trans. Carroll Mason Sparrow (Charlottesville: University of Virginia, 1947).

———, *Concerning The City of God against the Pagans*, ed. Henry Bettenson (New York: Penguin Books, 1980).

———, *De Natura Boni of Saint Augustine:* A Translation with an Introduction and Commentary, trans. and ed. A. Anthony Moon, (Washington, DC: Catholic University of America Press, 1955)

Aurobindo Ghose, Sri, *The Problem of Rebirth*, in *Sri Aurobindo Birth Centenary Library*, Vol. 16 (Pondicherry, India: Sri Aurobindo Ashram Trust, 1971).

Bakan, David, *Disease, Pain, and Sacrifice: Toward a Psychology of Suffering* (Chicago: University of Chicago Press, 1968).

Balthasar, Hans Urs von, *Dare We Hope That All Men Be Saved?* (San Francisco: Ignatius Press, 1988).

Bernstein, Alan E., *The Formation of Hell: Death and Retribution in the Ancient and Early Christian Worlds* (Ithaca, NY: Cornell University Press, 1993).

Berry, Thomas, et al., *Befriending the Earth: A Theology of Reconciliation between Humans and the Earth* (Mystic, CT: Twenty-Third Publications, 1991).

Blake, William, 'On Another's Sorrow', in *William Blake*, ed. J. Bronowski (New York: Viking Penguin, 1984).

Borg, Marcus, *Meeting Jesus Again for the First Time: The Historical Jesus and the Heart of Contemporary Faith* (New York: HarperSanFrancisco, 1995).

Botting, Heather, 'Medico-Scientific Assumptions Regarding Paradeath Phenomena: Explanation or Obfuscation', *Critical Reflections on the Paranormal*, eds. Michael Stoeber and Hugo Meynell (Albany, NY: SUNY Press, 1996), pp. 159–76.

Brown, Frank Burch, 'The Beauty of Hell: Anselm on God's Eternal Design', *Journal of Religion*, Vol. 73 (1993), 329–56.
Cassell, E. J., 'The Nature of Suffering and the Goals of Medicine,' *New England Journal of Medicine*, Vol. 306 (1982), 639–45.
Chignel, Andrew, 'Infant Suffering Revisited', *Religious Studies*, Vol. 37 (2001), 475–84.
_____, 'The Problem of Infant Suffering', *Religious Studies*, Vol. 34 (1998), 205–17.
Couture, André, *La Réincarnation au-delà des Idées reçues* (Paris: Éditions de l'Atelier/Éditions Ouvrières, 2000).
Crysdale, Cynthia, *Embracing Travail: Retrieving the Cross Today* (New York: Continuum, 1999).
Cuneo, Michael W., *American Exorcism: Expelling Demons in the Land of Plenty* (New York: Doubleday, 2001).
Cunningham, Lawrence S. and Egan, Keith J., *Christian Spirituality: Themes from the Tradition* (New York: Paulist Press, 1996).
Daly, Mary, *Beyond God the Father* (Boston: Beacon Press, 1973).
Davies, Oliver, *A Theology of Compassion: Metaphysics of Difference and the Renewal or Tradition* (Cambridge, MA: William B. Eerdmans, 2001).
Davis, Caroline Franks, *The Evidential Force of Religious Experience* (Oxford: Clarendon Press, 1989).
Day, Dorothy, *The Long Loneliness: The Autobiography of Dorothy Day* (New York: HarperSanFrancisco, 1997).
Dossy, Larry, 'The Return of Prayer', *Alternative Therapies*, Vol. 3, No. 6 (November 1997), 10–17, 113–20.
Dostoevsky, Fyodor, *The Brothers Karamazov*, the Garnett translation, revised by Ralph E. Matlaw (New York: W. W. Norton, 1976).
_____, *The Brothers Karamazov*, trans. Constance Garnett (New York: Modern Library, 1929).
Dupré, Louis, 'Evil – A Religious Mystery: A Plea For A More Inclusive Model of Theodicy', *Faith and Philosophy*, Vol. 7 (1990), 261–80.
_____, *Religious Mystery and Rational Reflection: Excursions in the Phenomenology and Philosophy of Religion* (Grand Rapids, MI: William B. Eerdmans, 1998).
Eckhart, Meister, *Breakthrough: Meister Eckhart's Creation Spirituality in New Translation*, ed. with commentary, Matthew Fox (New York: Image Books, 1980).
_____, *Meister Eckhart: Selected Treatises and Sermons Translated from Latin and German with an Introduction and Notes*, ed. James Clark and John V. Skinner (London, Faber & Faber 1958).
_____, *Meister Eckhart: Teacher and Preacher*, ed. Bernard McGinn, trans. Frank Tobin (New York: Paulist Press, 1986).
Edwards, Paul, 'The Case Against Reincarnation', *Free Inquiry*, Vol. 6, No. 4 (1986), 24–43, and Vol. 7, Nos 1–3 (1987), 38–48, 38–49, 46–53.
Evans, Donald D., 'Can Philosophers Limit What Mystics Can Do? A Critique of Steven Katz', *Religious Studies*, Vol. 25 (1989), 53–60.
_____, *The Logic of Self Involvement* (London: SCM Press, 1963).
_____, *Spirituality and Human Nature* (Albany, NY: SUNY Press, 1993).
Fiddes, Paul S., *The Creative Suffering of God* (Oxford: Oxford University Press, 1988).

Frankl, Viktor, *Man's Search for Meaning: An Introduction to Logotherapy*, 4th edn (Boston: Beacon Press, 1992).
Friedman, R.Z., 'Evil and moral agency', *Philosophy of Religion*, Vol. 24 (1988), 3–20.
Gluklich, Ariel, *Sacred Pain: Hurting the Body for the Sake of the Soul* (New York: Oxford University Press, 2001).
Grant, George, *Philosophy in the Mass Age* (Toronto: University of Toronto Press, 1995).
Guignon, Charles B. (ed.), *Dostoevsky: The Grand Inquisitor*, with related chapters from *The Brothers Karamazov* (Indianapolis: Hackett, 1993).
Gutiérrez, Gustavo, *A Theology of Liberation: History, Politics, and Salvation*, rev. and trans. Caridad Inda and John Eagleson (Maryknoll, NY: Orbis Books, 1988).
Hall, Douglas John, *The Cross in Our Context: Jesus and the Suffering World* (Minneapolis: Fortress Press, 2003).
Harrington, Daniel, *Why Do We Suffer? A Scriptural Approach to the Human Condition* (Franklin, WI: Sheed & Ward, 2000).
Heaney, John J., *The Sacred and the Psychic: Parapsychology and Christian Theology* (New York: Paulist Press, 1984).
Hick, John, *Death and Eternal Life* (Glasgow: William Collins, 1976).
_____, *Evil and the God of Love*, rev. edn (New York: HarperSanFrancisco, 1977).
Hügel, Baron F. von, 'What Do We Mean By Heaven? And What Do We Mean By Hell?' in *Essays and Addresses on the Philosophy of Religion*, Vol. I (London: J. M. Dent, 1921), pp. 195–224.
Irenaeus, St, *Irenaeus Against Heresies*, Vol. I of *The Ante-Nicene Fathers*, ed. Alexander Roberts and James Donaldson (Grand Rapids, MI: Wm. B. Eerdmans, 1979).
International Theological Commission, 'Some Current Questions in Eschatology', *Irish Theological Quarterly*, Vol. 58 (1992), 209–43.
Ivens, Michael, *Understanding the Spiritual Exercises: Text and Commentary, A Handbook for Retreat Directors* (Leominster, Herefordshire: Gracewing, 1998).
James, William, *The Varieties of Religious Experience: A Study in Human Nature* (New York: Collier Books, Macmillan, 1961).
Jantzen, Grace, *Becoming Divine: Towards a Feminist Philosophy of Religion* (Bloomington, IN: Indiana University Press, 1999).
_____, *Julian of Norwich: Mystic and Theologian* (New York: Paulist Press, 1988).
_____, *Power, Gender and Christian Mysticism* (Cambridge: Cambridge University Press, 1995).
John Paul II, Pope, *On the Christian Meaning of Human Suffering* (Boston, MA: St Paul Books & Media, 1984).
John Paul II, Pope, *On Human Work: Laborem Exercens* (Boston: Daughters of St Paul).
Johnson, Elizabeth A., *She Who Is: The Mystery of God in Feminist Theological Discourse* (New York: Crossroad, 2002).
Julian of Norwich, *Revelation of Love*, trans. John Skinner (New York: Image Books, 1997).
Jung, Karl, *Memories, Dreams, Reflections*, ed. Amiela Jaffe, trans. Richard and Clara Winston (New York: Vintage Books, 1963).

Katz, Richard, *Boiling Energy: Community Healing among the Kalahari Kung* (Cambridge, MA: Harvard University Press, 1982).
Kaufman, Whitley R. P., 'Karma, Rebirth, and the Problem of Evil', *Philosophy East & West*, Vol. 55 (2005) 15–32.
Kelsey, Morton T., *Healing and Christianity: In Ancient Thought and Modern Times* (New York: Harper & Row, 1973).
Klostermaier, Klaus K., *A Survey of Hinduism*, 2nd edn (Albany, NY: SUNY Press, 1994).
Kvanvig, Jonathan, *The Problem of Hell* (New York: Oxford University Press, 1993).
Lane, Dermot A., *Christ at the Centre: Selected Issues in Christology* (Dublin: Veritas Publications, 1990).
_____, *Keeping Hope Alive: Stirrings in Christian Theology* (New York: Paulist Press, 1996).
Latzer, Michael, 'The Nature of Evil: Leibniz and his Medieval Background,' *The Modern Schoolman*, Vol. 71 (1993) 59–69.
Lewis, C.S., *The Problem of Pain* (New York: Collier Books, Macmillan, 1962).
Lewis, C.S. (ed), *George MacDonald: An Anthology* (New York: Macmillan, 1948).
MacGregor, Geddes, *Reincarnation in Christianity: A New Vision of the Role of Rebirth in Christian Thought* (Wheaton, IL: Quest, 1978).
_____, *Reincarnation as a Christian Hope* (Totowa, NJ: Barnes & Noble, 1982).
Meier, John P., *A Marginal Jew: Rethinking the Historical Jesus*, Vol. II of *Mentor, Message, and Miracle* (New York: The Anchor Bible Reference Library, Doubleday, 1994).
Merton, Thomas, *New Seeds of Contemplation* (New York: New Directions Books, 1972).
Metz, Johann-Baptist., 'The Future in the Memory of Suffering', trans. John Griffiths, *New Questions on God*, an issue of *Concilium*, ed. Johann B. Metz, (New York: Herder & Herder, 1972), pp. 9–25.
_____, 'Suffering from God: Theology as Theodicy', *Pacifica*, Vol. 5 (1992), 274–87.
Mohammed, Ovey, 'Jesus and Krishna', *Journal of Ecumenical Studies*, Vol. 26 (1989), 664–80.
Morrison, Karl F., *'I am You': The Hermeneutics of Empathy in Western Literature, Theology, and Art* (Princeton: Princeton University Press, 1988).
Nayak, G. C., *Evil, Karma and Reincarnation* (Santiniketan, West Bengal: Centre of Advanced Study in Philosophy, Visva-Bharati, 1973).
Nelson, John E., *Healing the Split: Integrating Spirit into Our Understanding of the Mentally Ill*, rev. edn (Albany, NY: SUNY Press, 1994).
Nouwen, Henri J. M., *The Wounded Healer* (Toronto: Image Books, Doubleday, 1979).
Nouwen, Henri J. M., McNeill, Donald P. and Morrison, Douglas A., *Compassion: A Reflection on the Christian Life* (Toronto: Image Books, Doubleday, 1983).
Nussbaum, Martha, 'Compassion: The Basic Social Emotion', *Social Philosophy and Policy*, Vol. 13 (1996), 27–58.
O'Brien, David and Shannon, Thomas A. (eds), *Catholic Social Thought: The Documentary Heritage* (Maryknoll, NY: Orbis Books, 1992).
O'Connor, David, 'In Defense of Theoretical Theodicy', *Modern Theology*, Vol. 5 (1988), 61–74.

Origen, *Origen: An Exhortation to Martyrdom, Prayer, and Selected Works*, trans. Rowan A. Greer (New York: Paulist Press, 1979).
Outka, Gene, *Agape: An Ethical Analysis* (New Haven, CN: Yale University Press, 1972).
Peck, M. Scott, *People of the Lie: The Hope for Healing Human Evil* (New York: Touchstone, 1983).
Penelhum, Terence, 'Divine Goodness and the Problem of Evil', *The Problem of Evil*, ed. Marilyn McCord Adams and Robert Merrihew Adams (Oxford: Oxford University Press, 1990), pp. 69–82.
Petri, Asenath, *Individuality in Pain and Suffering*, 2nd edn (Chicago: University of Chicago Press, 1978).
Phan, Peter, 'Contemporary Context and Issues in Eschatology,' *Theological Studies*, Vol. 55 (1994), 507–36.
Pickering, George, *Creative Malady: Illness in the Lives and Minds of Charles Darwin, Florence Nightingale, Mary Baker Eddy, Sigmund Freud, Marcel Proust, Elizabeth Barrett Browning* (New York: Oxford University Press, 1974).
Pinnock, Sarah K., *Beyond Theodicy: Jewish and Christian Continental Thinkers Respond to the Holocaust* (Albany, NY: SUNY Press, 2002).
Plantinga, Alvin, *God, Freedom and Evil* (New York: Harper & Row, 1974).
Power, David N., 'Sacrament: Event Eventing,' in *A Promise of Presence*, ed. Michael Downey and Richard Fragomeni, (Washington, DC: Pastoral Press, 1992), pp. 271–99.
Principe, Walter, 'Toward Defining Spirituality', *Studies in Religion*, Vol. 12 (1983), 127–41.
Pytell, Timothy E., 'Redeeming the Unredeemable: Auschwitz and *Man's Search for Meaning*', *Holocaust and Genocide Studies*, Vol. 17 (2003), 89–113.
Rahner, Karl, *Foundations of Christian Faith: An Introduction to the Idea of Christianity*, trans. William V. Dych (New York: Seabury Press, 1978).
———, *The Practice of Faith: A Handbook of Contemporary Spirituality*, eds. Karl Lehmann and Albert Raffelt (New York: Crossroad, 1983).
———, 'Purgatory', *Faith and Ministry*, in Vol. 19 of *Theological Investigations*, trans. Edward Quinn (New York: Crossroad, 1983), pp. 181–93.
———, 'Why Does God Allow Us to Suffer?', *Faith and Ministry*, in Vol. 19 of *Theological Investigations*, trans. Edward Quinn (New York: Crossroad, 1983), pp. 205–08.
Rankka, Kristine M., *Women and the Value of Suffering: An Aw(e)ful Rowing Toward God* (Collegeville, MN: Michael Glazier, Liturgical Press, 1998).
Ricoeur, Paul, 'Evil, A Challenge to Philosophy and Theology', trans. David Pellauer, *Journal of the American Academy of Religion*, Vol. 53 (1985), 635–48.
Rilke, Rainer Maria, *Letters To A Young Poet*, trans. Stephen Mitchell (New York: Vintage Books, 1984).
Sachs, John R., 'Current Eschatology: Universal Salvation and the Problem of Evil', *Theological Studies*, Vol. 52 (1991), 227–54.
———, 'Resurrection or Reincarnation? The Christian Doctrine of Purgatory', *Reincarnation or Resurrection?*, an issue of *Concilium*, ed. Herman Häring and Johann-Baptist Metz (London: SCM Press 1993), pp. 81–7.
Sayers, Dorothy L., 'Introduction to *The Comedy of Dante Alighieri The Florentine, Cantica II: Purgatory* (1955; Harmondsworth: Penguin Books, 1981).
Scholem, Gershom, *Kabbalah* (New York: Meridian Books, 1978).

Schneiders, Sandra M., 'Spirituality in the Academy', *Theological Studies*, Vol. 50 (1989), 676–97.
Scott, Michael, 'The Morality of Theodicies', *Religious Studies*, Vol. 32 (1996), 1–13.
Dorothee Soelle, *The Silent Cry: Mysticism and Resistance* (Minneapolis: Fortress, 2001).
_____, *Suffering*, trans. Everett R. Kalin (Philadelphia: Fortress, 1975).
_____ with Cloyes, Shirley A., *To Work and To Love: A Theology of Creation* (Philadelphia: Fortress, 1984).
Stein, Edith, *On the Problem of Empathy*, trans. Waltraut Stein, 3rd edn, Vol. 3 of *The Collected Works of Edith Stein* (Washington, DC: ICS, 1989).
Stevenson, Ian, *Children Who Remember Previous Lives: A Question of Reincarnation* (Charlottesville: University Press of Virginia, 1987).
Stewart, Kilton, *Pygmies and Dream Giants* (New York: Harper Colophon Books, 1975).
Stoeber, Michael, *Evil and the Mystics' God: Towards A Mystical Theodicy* (Toronto: University of Toronto Press, 1992).
_____, 'Hell, Divine Love, and Divine Justice', *Logos*, Vol. 2 (1999), 176–99.
_____, 'Personal Identity and Rebirth,' *Religious Studies*, Vol. 26 (1990), 493–500.
_____, *Theo-Monistic Mysticism: A Hindu–Christian Comparison* (London: Macmillan, 1994).
_____, 'Transformative Suffering, Destructive Suffering, and the Question of Abandoning Theodicy', *Studies in Religion*, Vol. 32 (2003), 429–47.
Stuart, James (trans and ed), *Swāmī Abhishiktānanda: His Life Told through His Letters* (Delhi: ISPCK, 1989).
Stump, Eleanor, 'Aquinas on the Sufferings of Job', *Reasoned Faith: Essays in Philosophical Theology in Honor of Norman Kretzmann*, ed. Eleanor Stump (Ithaca, NY: Cornell University Press, 1993), pp. 328–57.
Suchocki, Marjorie Hewitt, *The Fall to Violence: Original Sin in Relational Theology* (New York: Continuum, 1994).
Surin, Kenneth, *Theology and the Problem of Evil* (Oxford: Blackwell, 1986).
Thiel, John E., *God, Evil and Innocent Suffering: A Theological Reflection* (New York: Crossroad, 2002).
Thomas Aquinas, St, *On Evil*, trans. Jean Oesterle (Notre Dame, IN: University of Notre Dame Press, 1995).
Tilley, Maureen A. and Ross, Susan A. (eds), *Broken and Whole: Essays on Religion and the Body* (Lanham, MD: University Press of America, 1995).
Tilley, Terence, *The Evils of Theodicy* (Washington, DC: Georgetown University Press, 1991).
Tillich, Paul, *Systematic Theology*, Vol. 3 (Chicago: University of Chicago Press, 1963).
Toolan, David S., 'Reincarnation and Modern Gnosis', *Reincarnation or Resurrection?*, an issue of *Concilium*, ed. Herman Häring and Johann-Baptist Metz (London: SCM Press, 1993), pp. 32–45.
Tournier, Paul, *Creative Suffering*, trans. Edwin Hudson (New York: Harper & Row, 1982).
Turner, Alice K., *The History of Hell* (New York: Harcourt Brace, 1993).
Trigg, Joseph Wilson, *Origen: The Bible and Philosophy in the Third-century Church* (Atlanta: John Knox Press, 1983).

Underhill, Evelyn, *Fragments from an Inner Life*, ed. Dana Greene (Harrisburg, PA: Morehouse Publishing, 1993).
Valiente-Noailles, Carlos, *The Kua: Life and Soul of the Central Kalahari Bushmen* (Brookfield, VT: Balkema, 1993).
Vanier, Jean, *Becoming Human* (Toronto: House of Anansi Press, 1998).
Ward, Keith, *Religion and Human Nature* (Oxford: Clarendon Press, 1998).
Washburn, Michael, *The Ego and the Dynamic Ground: A Transpersonal Theory of Human Development* (Albany, NY: SUNY Press, 1988).
Weil, Simone, 'The Love of God and Affliction', *Simone Weil: Writings, Selected with an Introduction*, ed. Eric O. Springsted (Mayknoll, NY: Orbis Books, 1998)
Wetzel, James, 'Can Theodicy be Avoided? The Claim of Unredeemed Evil', *Religious Studies*, Vol. 25 (1989), 1–13.
White, Jr, Lynn, 'The Historical Roots of our Ecological Crisis', *Science*, Vol. 155, No. 3767 (March 1967), as reprinted in *The Christian Difference* (Needham Heights, MA: Pearson Custom, 1999), pp. 400–8.
Wiebe, Phillip H., *God and Other Spirits: Intimations of Transcendence in Christian Experience* (New York: Oxford University Press, 2004).
Wiseman, James A., '"Enveloped by Mystery": The Spiritual Journey of Henri Le Saux/Abhishiktānanda', *Église et Théologie*, Vol. 23 (1992), 241–60.
Wood, James, 'Twister', *The New Republic*, Vol. 218, No. 23 (June 1998), 46.
Yandell, Keith E. 'The Doctrine of Hell and Moral Philosophy', *Religious Studies*, Vol. 28 (1992), 75–90.
Zaleski, Carol, *The Life of the World to Come: Near-Death Experience and Christian Hope* (New York: Oxford University Press, 1996).
———, *Otherworldly Journeys: Accounts of Near-Death Experience in Medieval and Modern Times* (New York: Oxford University Press, 1987).

Index

Abhishiktānanda (Henri Le Saux) 48, 113n27
Adams, M.M. 61, 93–4, 115n58, 116n1, 119n26
afterlife beliefs
  significance for theodicy x, 11–12, 15, 58, 73, 75–7, 80–101, 119n25, 119n26
  see also heaven, hell, purgatory, rebirth, universal salvation
Allen, D. 116n1, 117n2
Anointing of the Sick 76, 120n29
apathy 14, 35–8, 72–3, 77, 81–2, 88, 90–1, 97, 99, 100, 101
Augustine, St 76, 84–7, 90, 119n28, 121n11, 123n26
Aurobindo Ghose, Sri 97–8, 127n41

Balthasar, H.U. von 121n8, 122n17, 126n37
Blake, W. 13, 34–5, 121n1
Bodhisattva 98
Boeme, J. 117n2
Book of Genesis 9–10, 18, 42–3
Book of Job 82
Borg, M. 36, 39–40, 120n1
Botting, H. 131n46
Brothers Karamazov, The 3–6, 10, 38, 46–8, 55–8, 62–3, 67–9, 72–3, 76–7, 83–4, 86, 90, 94, 103n9

Cassel, E.J. 105n4, 105n5, 108n28
Catholic Worker, The 111n13
Chignell, A. 127n41
'Christian Hermeticist, The' 30, 32, 50, 110n35, 127n41, 130n45
compassion
  and mercy 120n1
  and pity 29, 38
  and prayer 26, 107n20
  as a response to suffering x, 2, 4, 9, 12, 22–3, 26, 28–9, 31–2, 35, 37–9, 41, 44–5, 48, 51, 72, 75, 81, 88
  defined 26–30, 108n31, 111n8
  for non-human creation 41–4, 48, 55–6, 101, 112n16
  in the Bible 120n1
  of Christians and atheists 44–6, 54
  of God 4, 7, 9, 13, 45, 48, 50, 52, 121n1
  of Jesus Christ ix, 13, 30–1, 36, 39, 44, 50–4, 89, 101, 113n27
  politics of ix, 14, 39–41, 43–4, 101, 111n8
contemplation 49, 51–3
Crysdale, C. 132n49
Cuneo, M. 25–6, 106n16, 107n19
Cunningham, L. 106n8.

Davies, O. 109n31
Day, D. 111n13
deism 13, 103n9
Dossy, L. 107n20
Dostoevsky, F. x, 3, 10, 46–7, 54–5, 83, 94
Dupré, L. x, 6, 14, 44, 49, 68, 103n9

ecological/environment issues 41–4, 55, 112n16
Eckhart, Meister J. 49, 52, 54, 56, 89
Edwards, P. 128n44
Egan, K. 106n8

140

empathy
  and compassion   14, 27,
    29–32, 35, 37–9, 45, 49, 70,
    72, 99–100, 110n6
  defined   27, 29, 137
  distorted forms of   14, 32,
    35–9, 49, 72, 77, 91, 97,
    99–100, 110n6, 113n25
eucharist   47–8, 51, 53–4
Evans, D.   25, 88, 100, 106n17,
    109n33, 122n18, 123n25
exorcism   25–6, 106n16,
    107n19

feminist theology   41, 63–4,
    112n14
Fiddes, P.   113n27
Francis of Assisi, St   43
Frankl, V.   28, 107n25

God   see compassion, Jesus
    Christ, suffering
Glucklich, A.   108n28
Gutiérrez, G.   111n13

Harrington, D.   105n2
Hawkes-Teeples, S.   120n1
healing
  hope of   ix–x, 19, 43, 66–8,
    74–8, 81–2, 92–101,
    128n44, 132n46
  practices and ministries of
    2–3, 21–31, 53, 75, 104n9,
    107n20, 110n37, 113n25,
    113n27, 115n58, 117n2,
    119n26, 120n29, 120n31
  see also Jesus Christ
heaven   15, 87, 89, 90, 99,
    123n24
hell   15, 71, 78, 81–8, 90–2, 94,
    98–9, 101, 123n26, 124n34
Hick, J.   x, 20–1, 84–5, 104n12,
    105n5, 119n26, 126n37,
    131n45
Holocaust   28, 60, 69, 97,
    107n25
Hügel, Baron F. von   89–91, 95,
    123n22, 123n24
Hugh of St Victor   87, 90

Ignatius of Loyola, St   51, 54
Irenaeus, St   91, 123n26

Jantzen, G.   63–4, 112n14
Jesus Christ
  and miracles   110n37
  and spiritual experience
    47–56, 113n27
  as exemplar   ix, 13–14, 39, 44,
    46, 89
  as healer   30, 31, 35–6, 60, 75,
    110n37, 113n27
  as mother   51
  as redeemer   5–6, 44, 47–9, 51,
    53
  as shaman   31–2, 52
  compassion of   ix, 30–1, 36,
    50–4, 101, 113n27
  Passion and Resurrection of
    ix, 5–6, 14, 31–2, 36, 44–8,
    54, 68, 80, 104n12, 114n27
  suffering of   18, 32, 44–58,
    113n27
John Paul II   28, 40, 49, 108n29
Julian of Norwich   50–1, 54,
    104n11
Jung, K.   25, 30
justice   5, 7, 32, 40, 86, 92, 95,
    100

Kabbalah   127n41
Kaufman, W.   128n44
Kelsey, M.   25, 35–6, 76, 104n9,
    110n37, 113n25, 120n29
kenosis   46–7, 54–5
Kung people   22–3, 25–8, 31,
    106n9
Kvanig, J.   121n3

Lane, D.   45–6, 96, 113n27,
    116n59, 124n27, 129n45
Latzer, M.   120n28
liberation theology   41, 111n13

MacGregor, G.   126n37, 127n41
Maurin, P.   111n13
Marcel, G.   123n25
Maskulak, M.   43

masochism 14, 32, 37–9, 45, 81–2, 90, 100, 101, 113n25
Meier, J. 110n37
Merton, T. 49, 53–4
Mohammed, O. xi, 129n45
mysticism 8, 49–55, 62, 102n7, 122n19
mystic-saints 14, 56–7, 69, 89, 90

narcissism 20–2, 45, 47, 50, 61, 69, 81, 88–9
Nayak, G. 127n39
Negrito people 23–8, 31
Nelson, J. 27, 29
Nouwen, H. 31, 48, 110n39
Nussbaum, M. 29, 108n31, 111n8

Origen 85, 125n37

Paul, St 29, 35–6, 47, 80, 109n33
Peck, M.S. 25, 106n17
Penelhum, T. 12
Phan, P. 88, 122n13, 125n37
Pinnock, S. 118n16
Plantinga, A. 104n10
Power, D. 47
prayer 26, 107n20
process theology 110n6, 113n21
punishment
  reformative 95–8, 100
  retributive 75–6, 82–8, 90–2, 98, 100, 119n28, 120n29, 121n11
  see also hell
purgatory 15, 73, 76, 78, 82–3, 94–7, 99, 120n31, 124n32, 124n34, 124n35, 124n36, 125n37, 126n38, 127n41, 128n45, 131n46
Pytell, T. 107n25

Rahner, K. 122n17, 122n19, 124n32, 125n37, 126n37, 128n45
rebirth, reincarnation 15, 73, 78, 82–3, 94–5, 97–9, 120n31, 127n40, 127n41, 128n44, 128n45, 131n46
Ricoeur, P. 29
Rilke, R.M. 28–9

Sachs, J. 121n8, 124n36
sadism 14, 32, 37–9, 81–2, 87, 90, 100–101
Sayers, D. 95–6, 124n34
Scholem, G. 127n41
sin 20–2, 45, 47, 61, 69, 81, 88–101, 119n28, 120n29, 121n11, 123n24, 123n25, 123n26, 124n34, 124n35, 125n37, 127n40,
Smith, P. 105n3
Soelle, D. ix, 18, 28, 32, 36, 40, 45–6, 53–4, 56, 62, 67–8, 70, 82, 100–101
spiritual experience
  and theodicy 13–14, 102n7, 102n8, 103n9
  nature of 6–15
  see also contemplation, mysticism, Jesus Christ
spirituality
  and transformation 9–11, 20–1, 26–31, 104n12
  Christian 106n8
  defined 20–1, 106n8
Stein, E., St 27, 43
Stevenson, I. 131n46
Stoeber, M. 102n8, 116n65, 117n2, 124n27, 127n41
Stump, E. 115n58
Suchocki, M. 110n6, 113n21
suffering
  destructive ix, x, 2, 5, 9–13, 15, 19, 39, 41, 44, 56–8, 60–78, 81–2, 92–5, 116n1, 116n2, 119n26
  in Christian scripture 18–19, 105n2
  of children 2–5, 57–8, 60, 77, 92–3, 95–7
  of Christ 18, 44–58, 113n27
  transformative viii, ix, 9, 11, 15, 18–32, 45, 61–2, 65, 69–70, 73–5, 81–2, 91, 94,

98, 101, 105n2, 105n3, 108n28, 116n2
Surin, K.   64–7, 75, 102n1, 118n15, 119n25

theodicy
  and afterlife possibilities   72–8, 80–101, 119n25, 119n26
  and Jesus Christ   5–6, 9, 31–2, 44–56
  defined   viii, 6, 102n1
  free will theme   10–13, 71–2, 77, 86, 89, 92–5, 99
  issues of   2–6, 56–8, 63–8, 102n1, 118n15
  practical theodicy   65, 118n17
  soul-making   ix, 10–12, 77, 97–9, 104n112, 128n44
  spiritual framework of   9–15, 68–72

Thiel, J.   118n16
Thomas Aquinas, St   76, 119n28, 120n29
Tilley, T.   63, 102n1
Tillich, P.   124n35, 126n38
Trigg, J.W.   126n37
Toolan, D.   124n41

Underhill, E.   53–4
universal salvation   15, 61, 71, 84–5, 88, 94, 99, 122n17

Vanier, J.   92–4

Ward, K.   126n37, 132n46
Weil, S.   53, 61, 94, 116n2
Wetzel, J.   118n17
White, L.   42–3
work   19, 40–1, 111n9

Zwerner, J.M.   104n12, 108n28